YOU AND ME

A Book of Friendship, Love and Kindness

JANG AND FOX

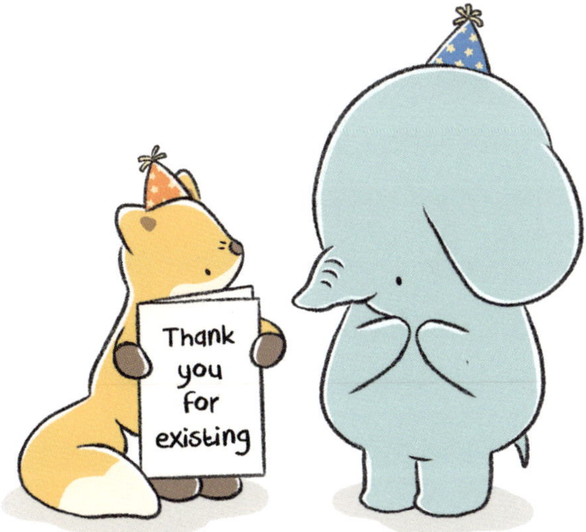

HarperCollinsPublishers

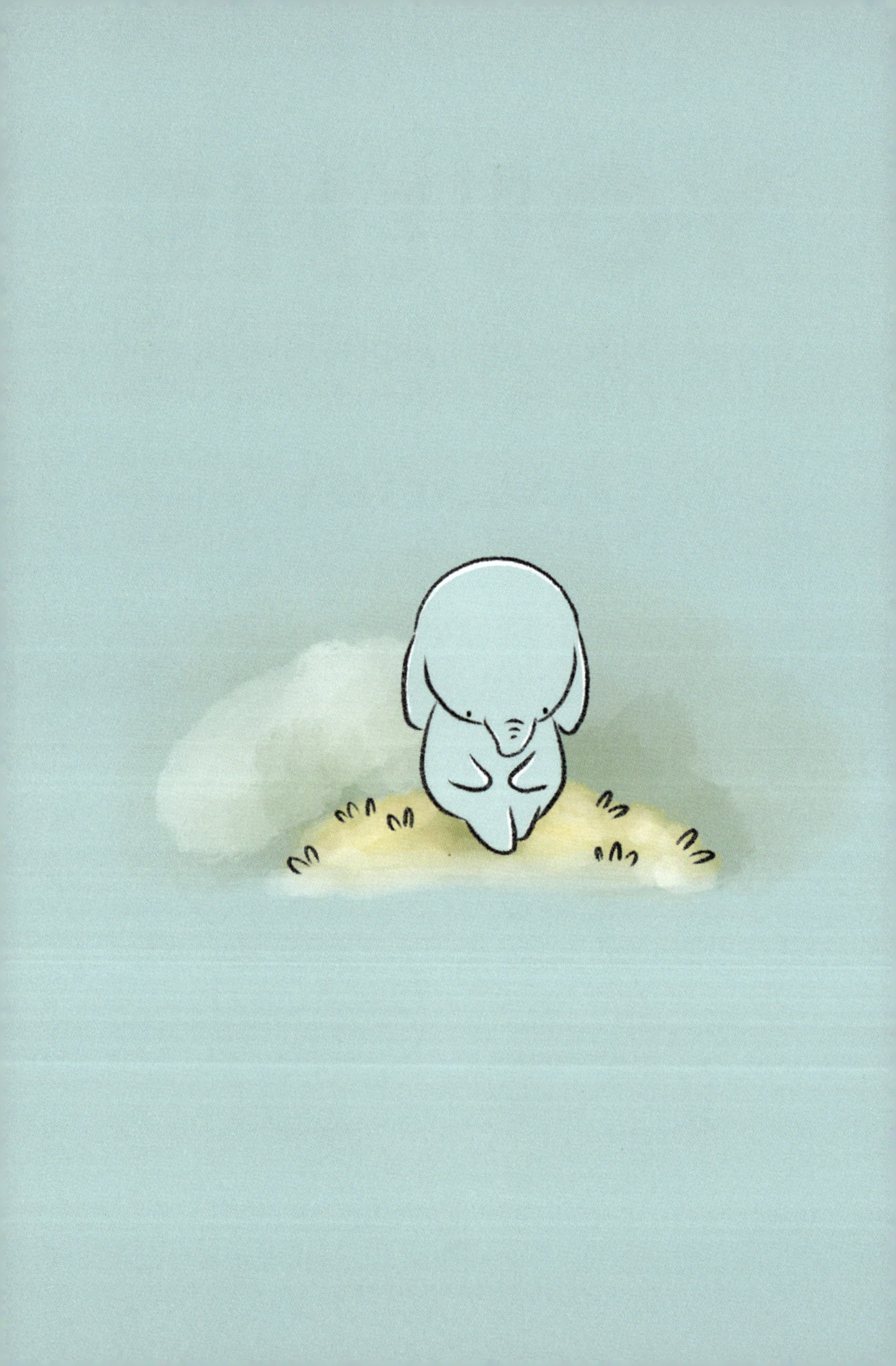

CONTENTS

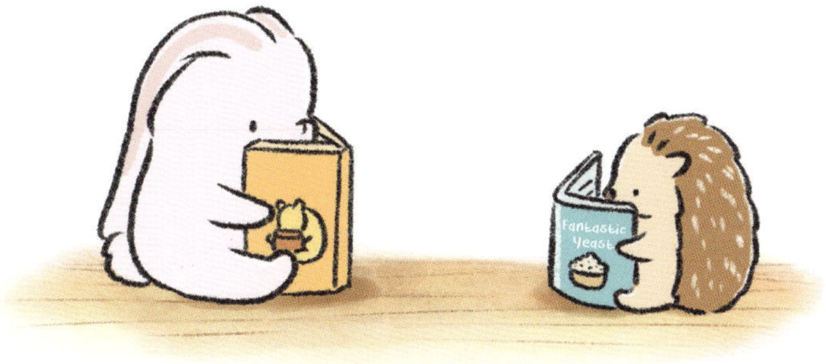

Rain or Shine

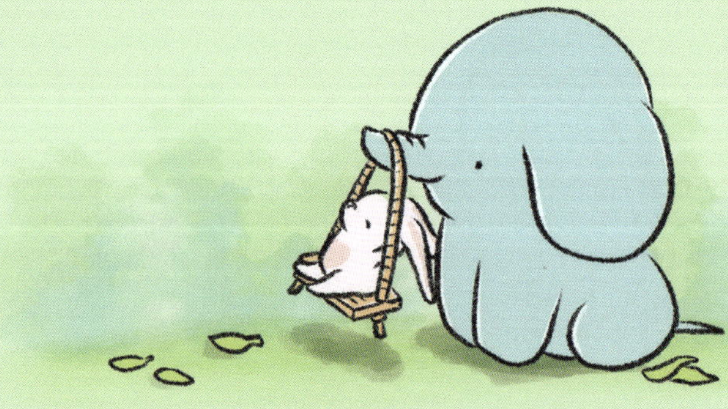

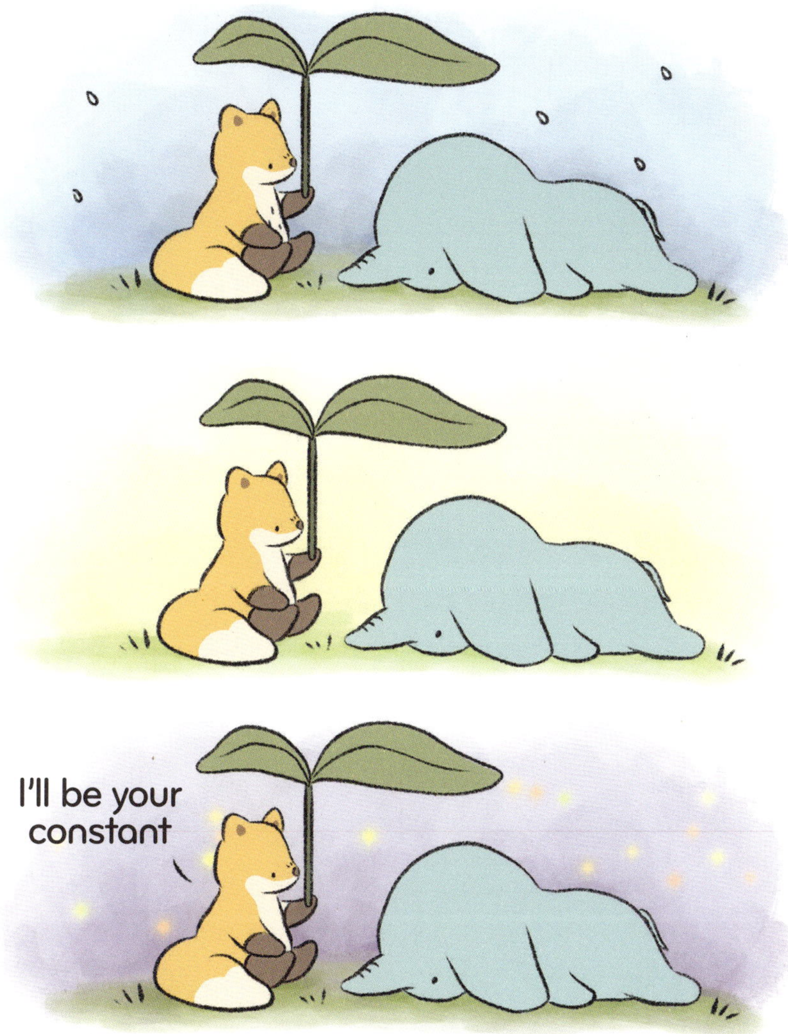
I'll be your constant

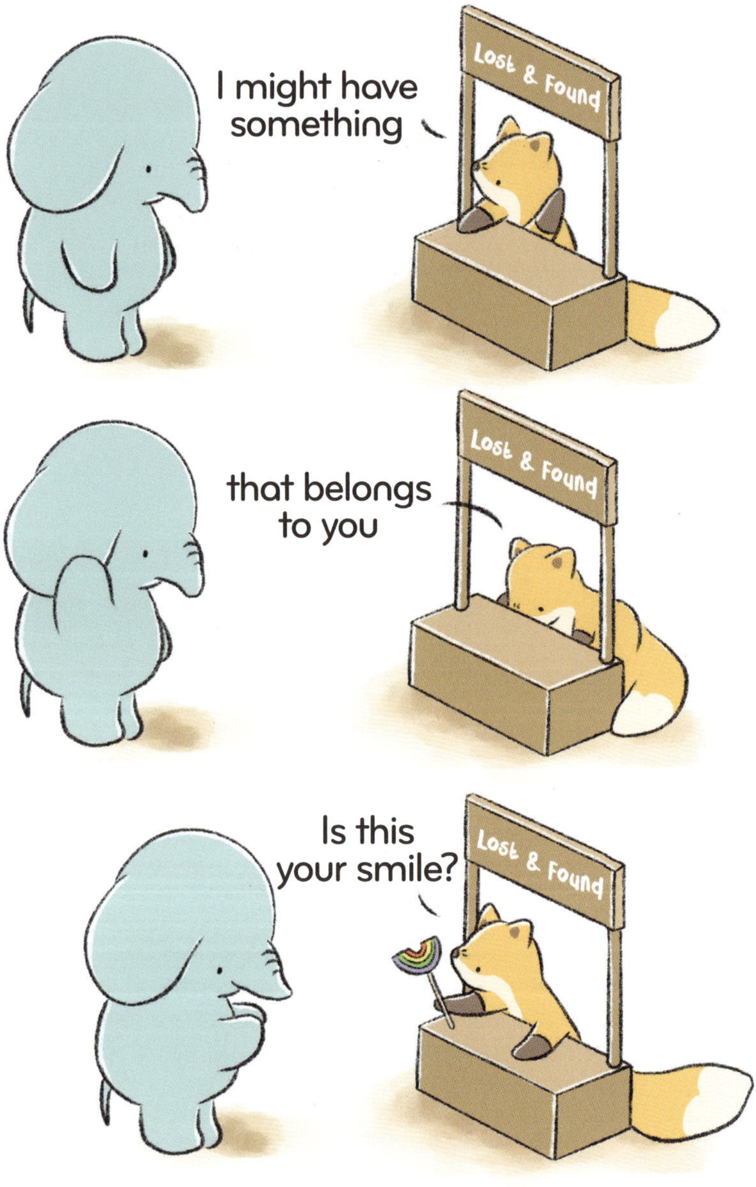
Lost & Found
I might have something
Lost & Found
that belongs to you
Lost & Found
Is this your smile?

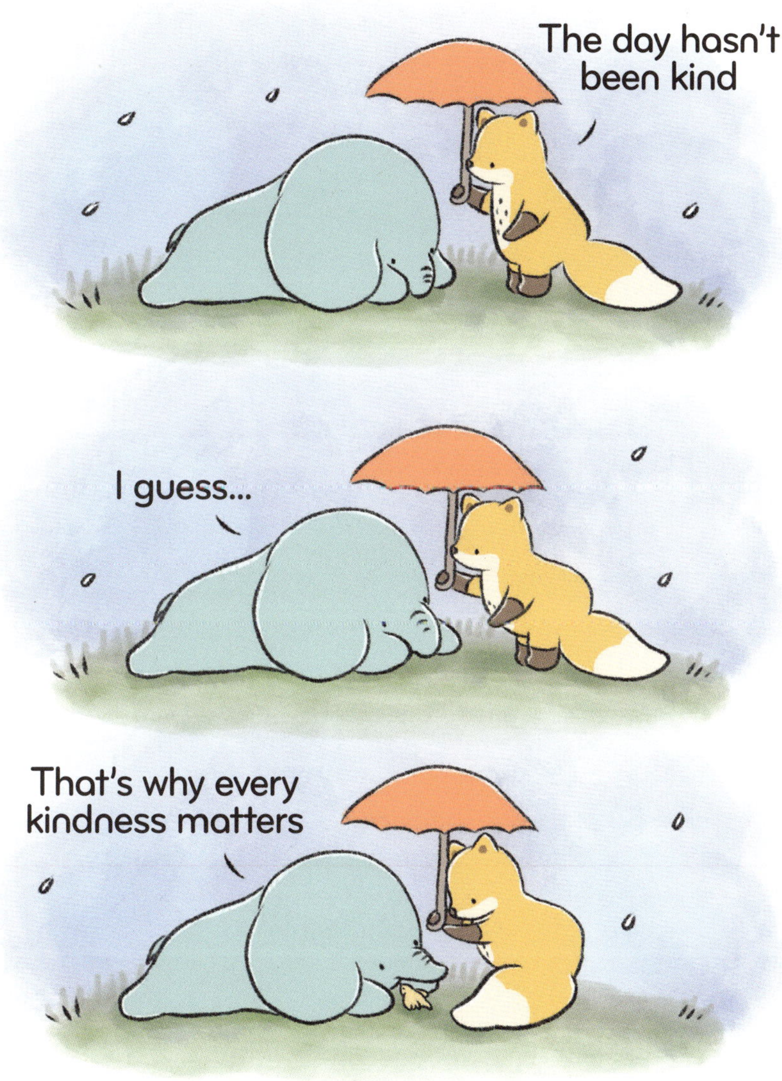
The day hasn't been kind
I guess...
That's why every kindness matters

On the days you feel invisible

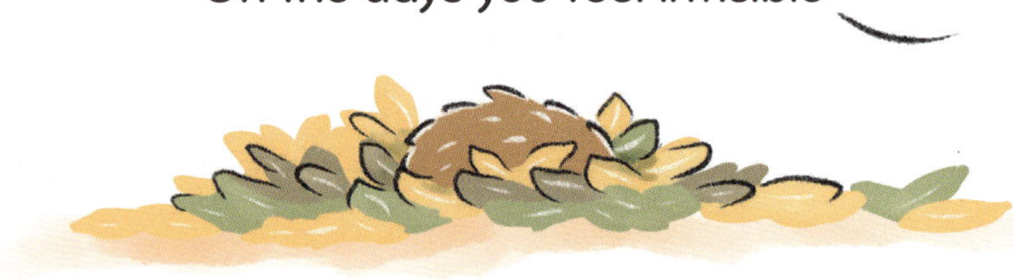

remember that
you're a treasure

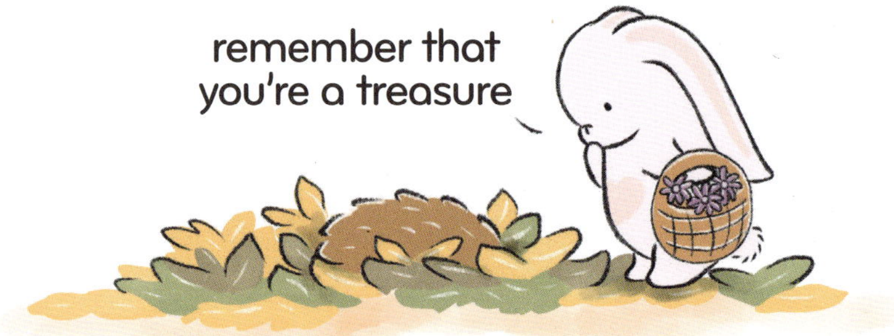

to someone!

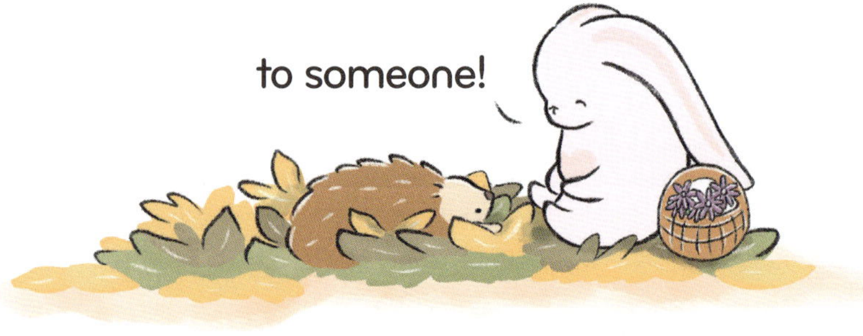

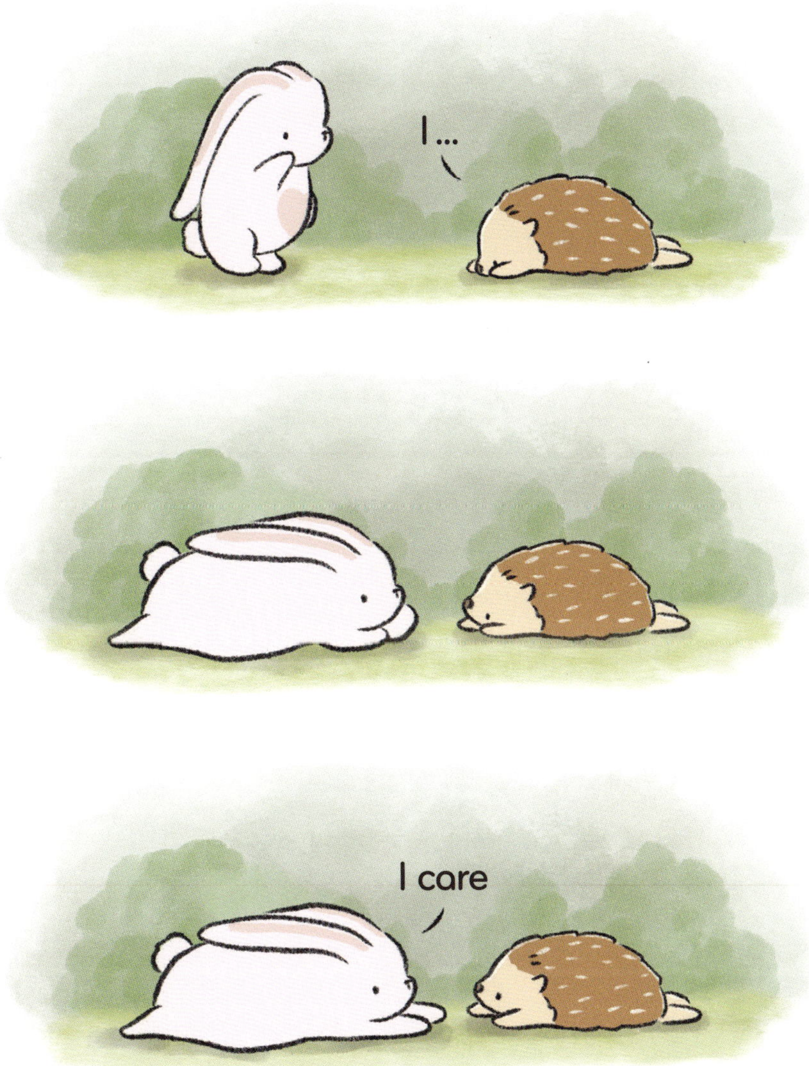
I...
I care

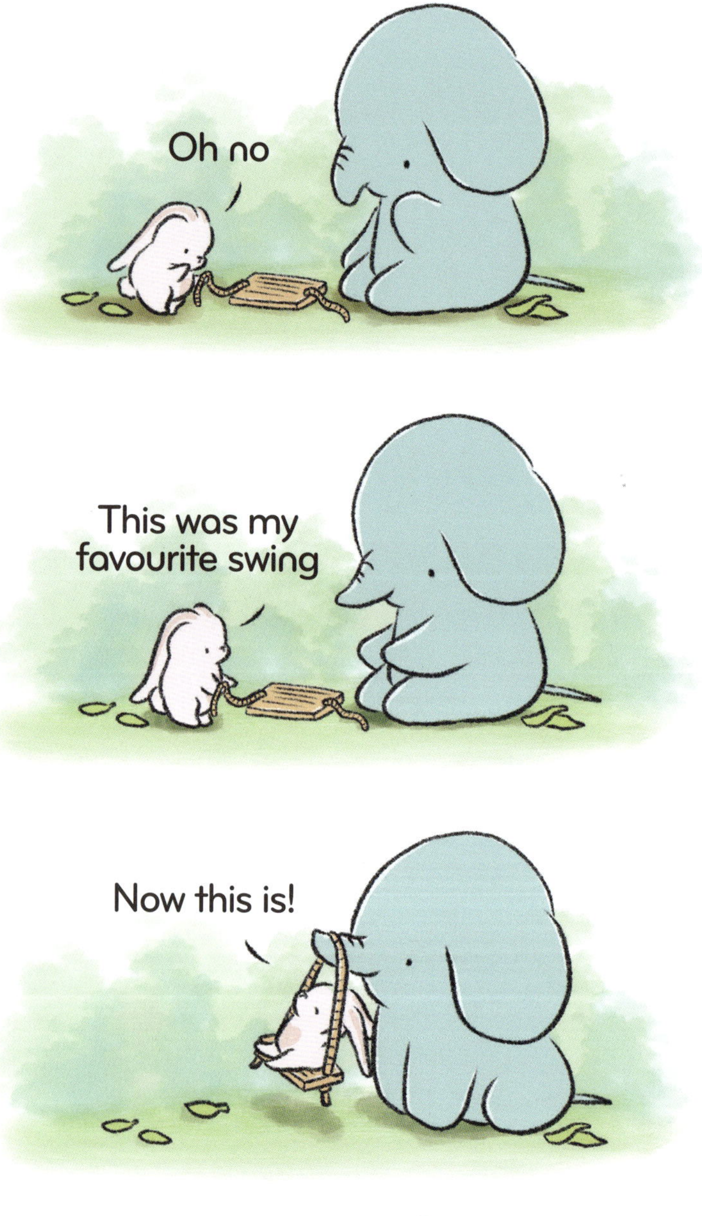
Oh no
This was my favourite swing
Now this is!

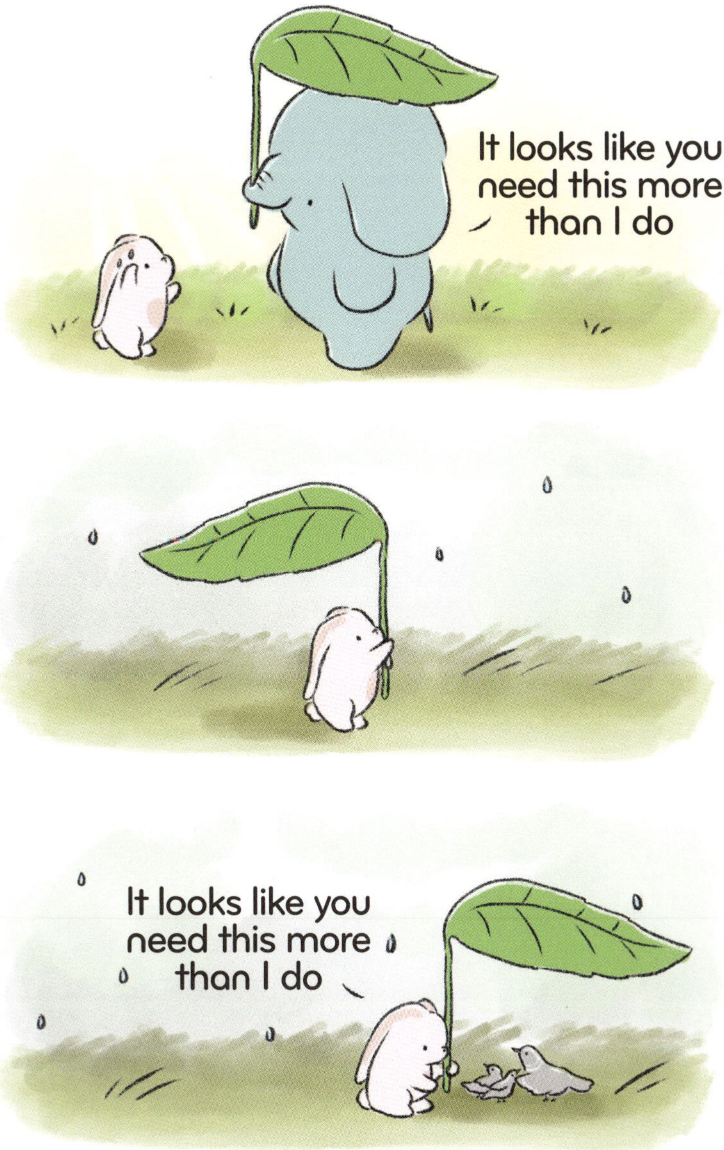
It looks like you need this more than I do
It looks like you need this more than I do

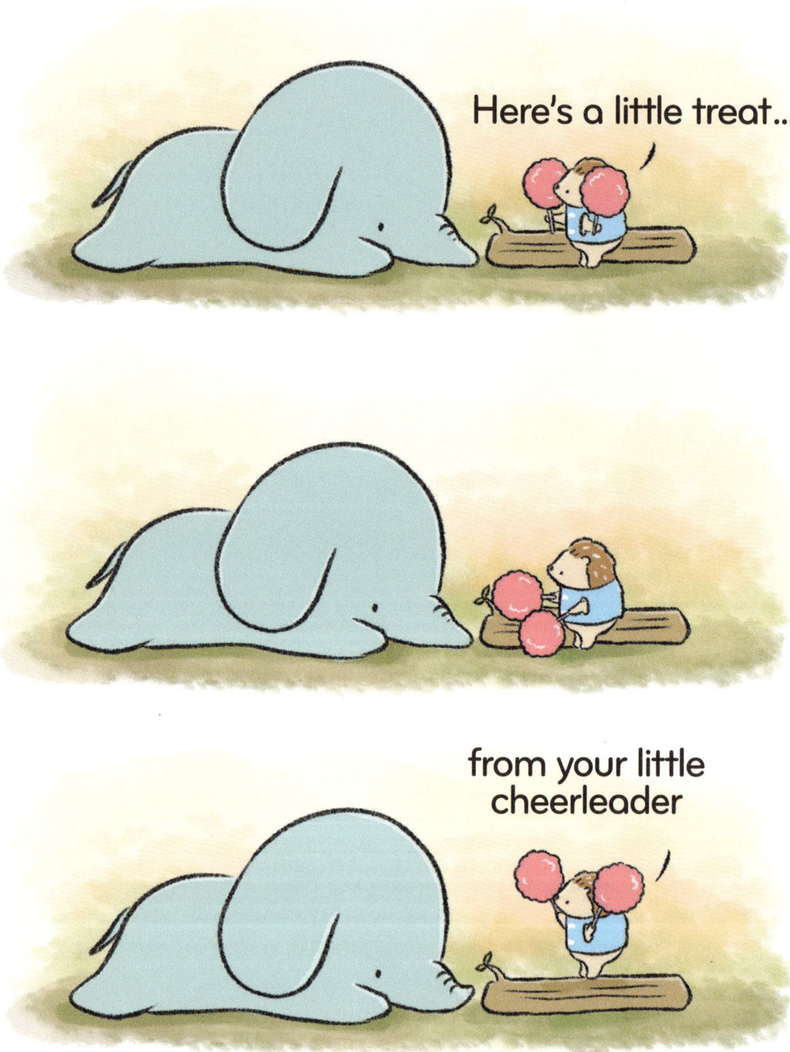
Here's a little treat...
from your little cheerleader

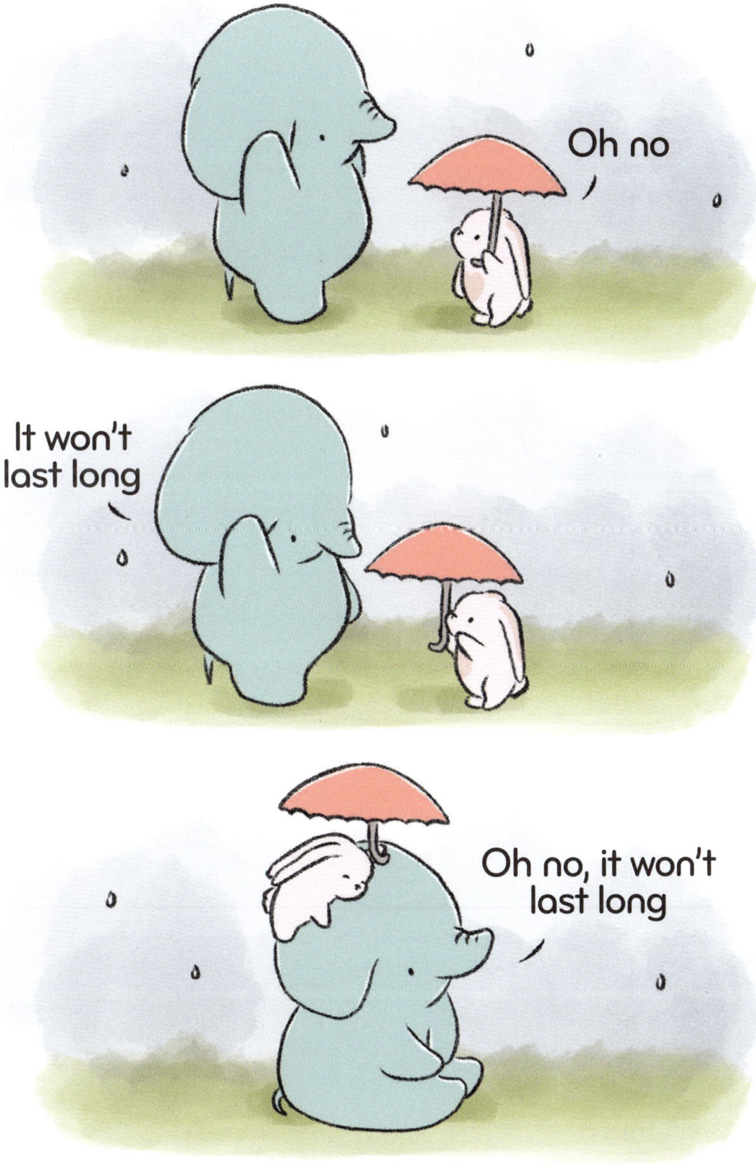

Oh no
It won't last long
Oh no, it won't last long

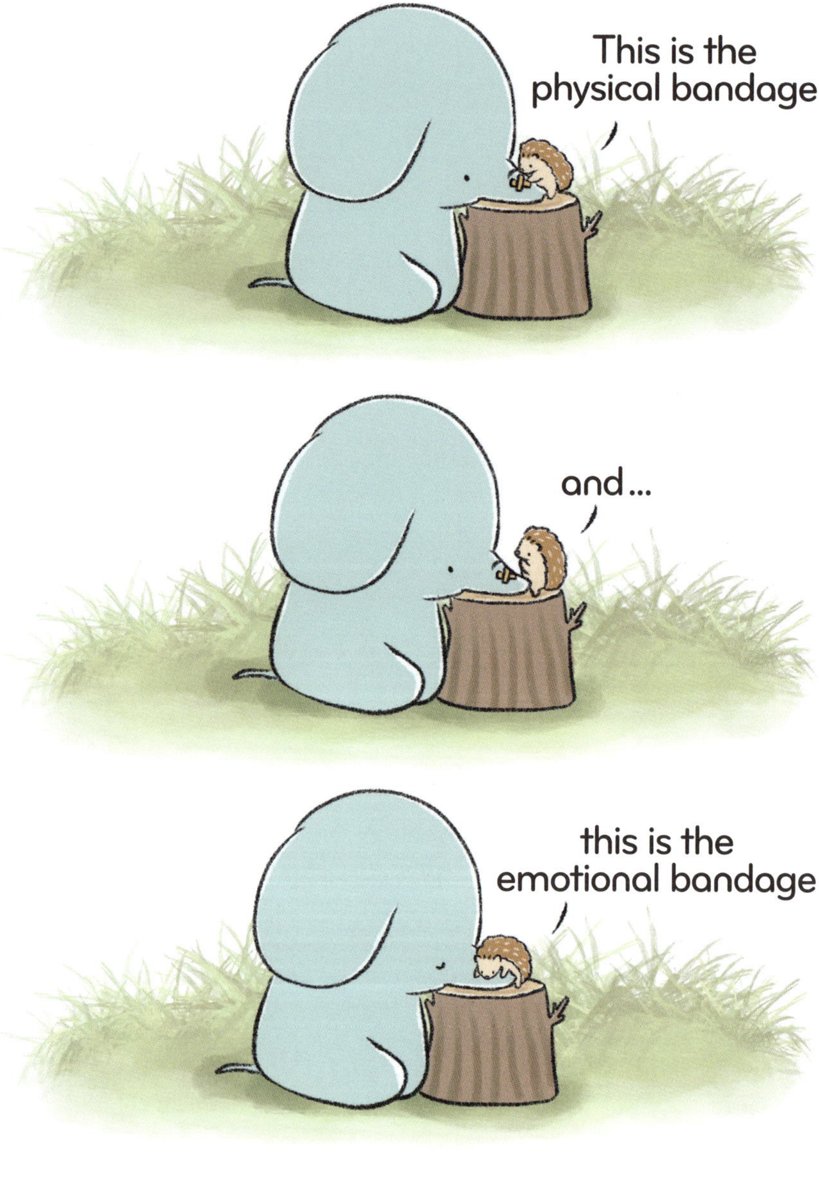
This is the physical bandage
and...
this is the emotional bandage

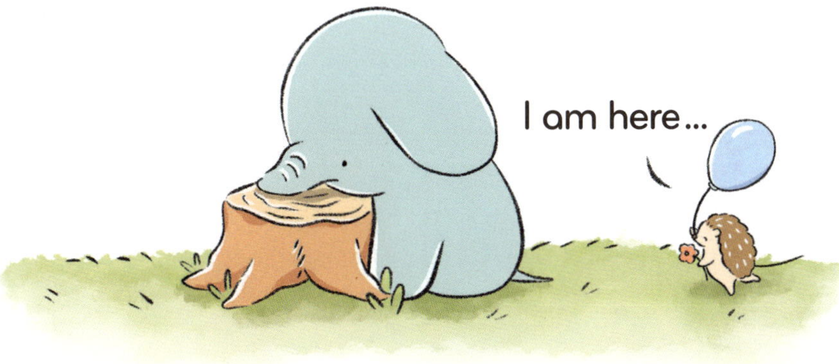
I am here...

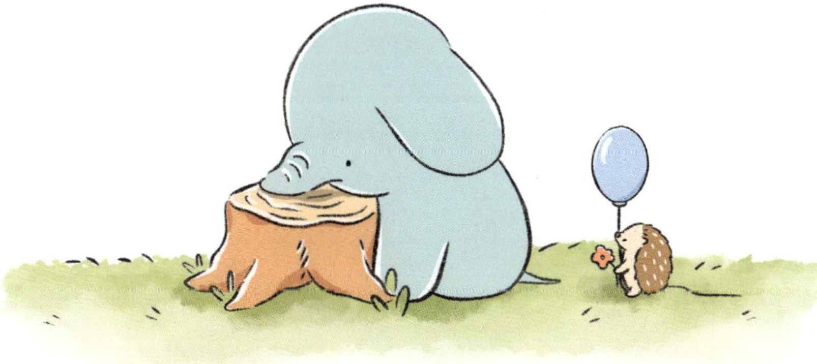

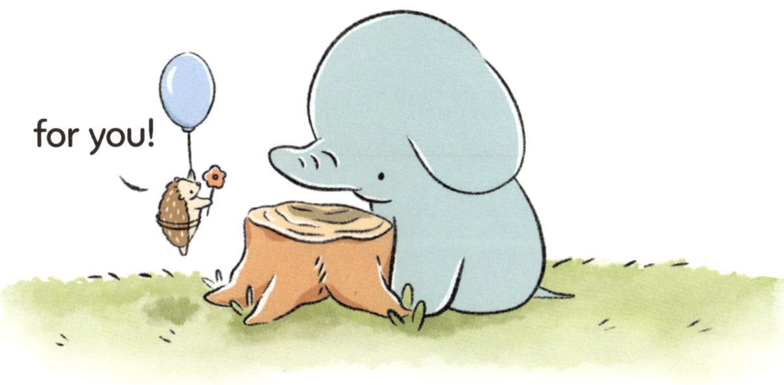
for you!

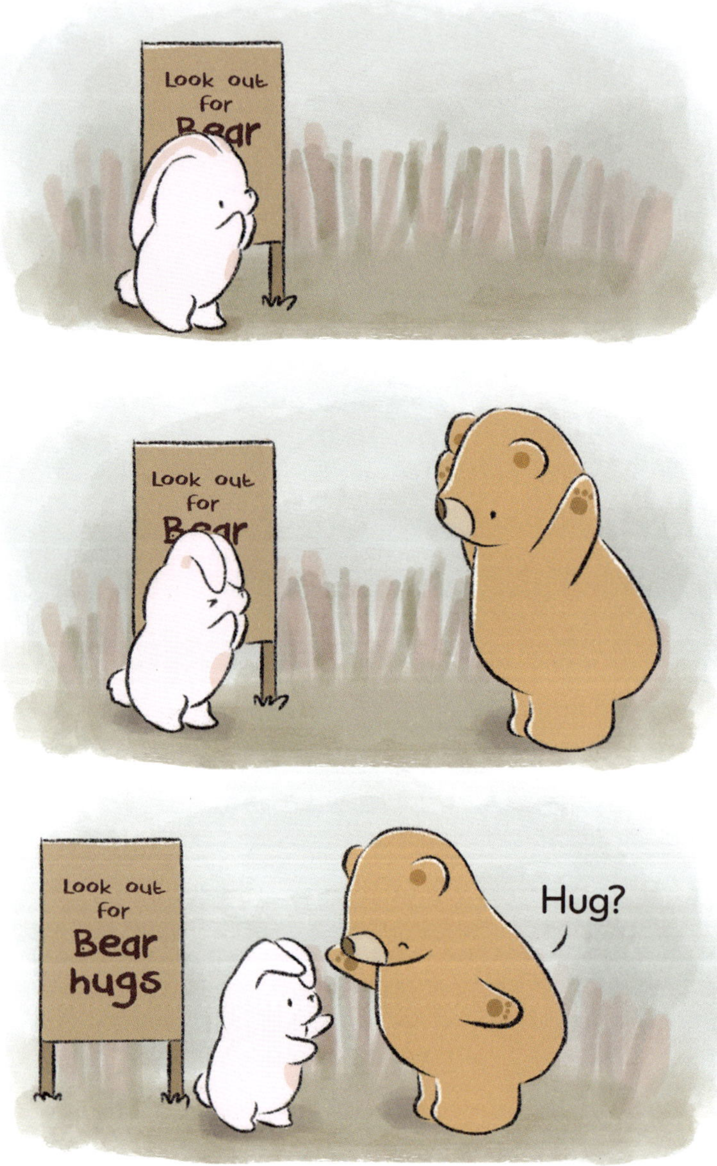
Look out for
Look out for
Look out for Bear hugs
Hug?

At the end

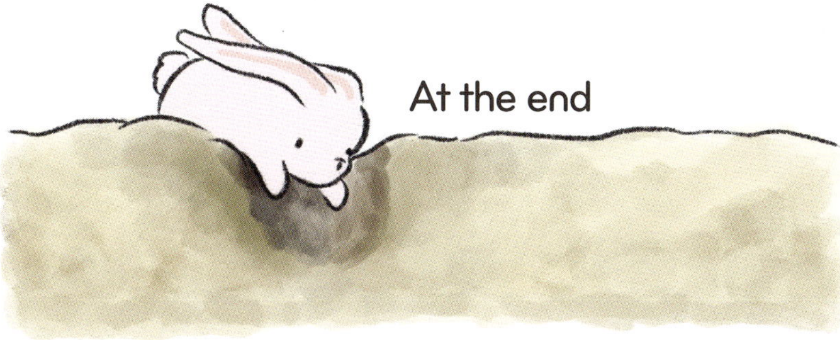

of the day...

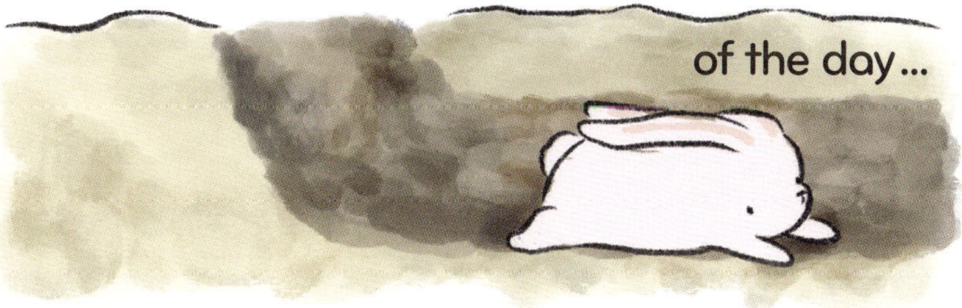

I will find my way to you

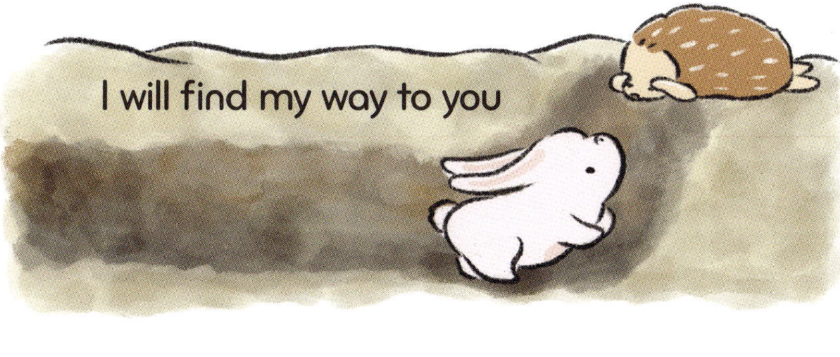

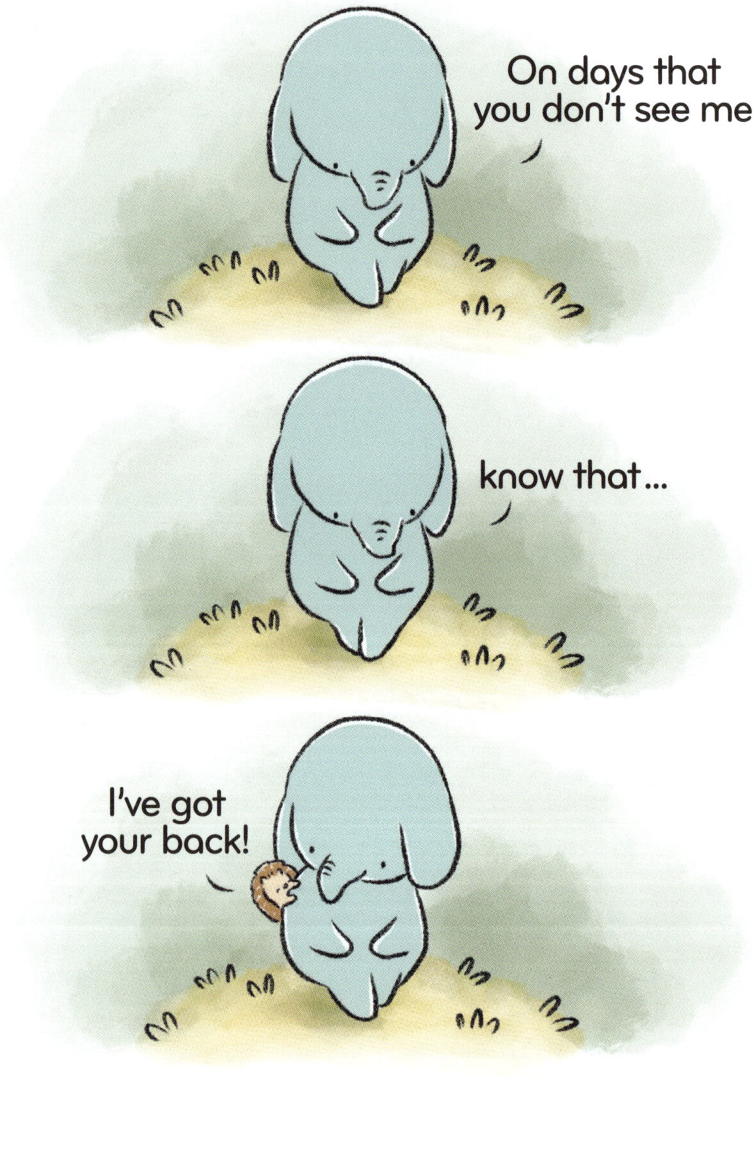
On days that
you don't see me
know that...
I've got
your back!

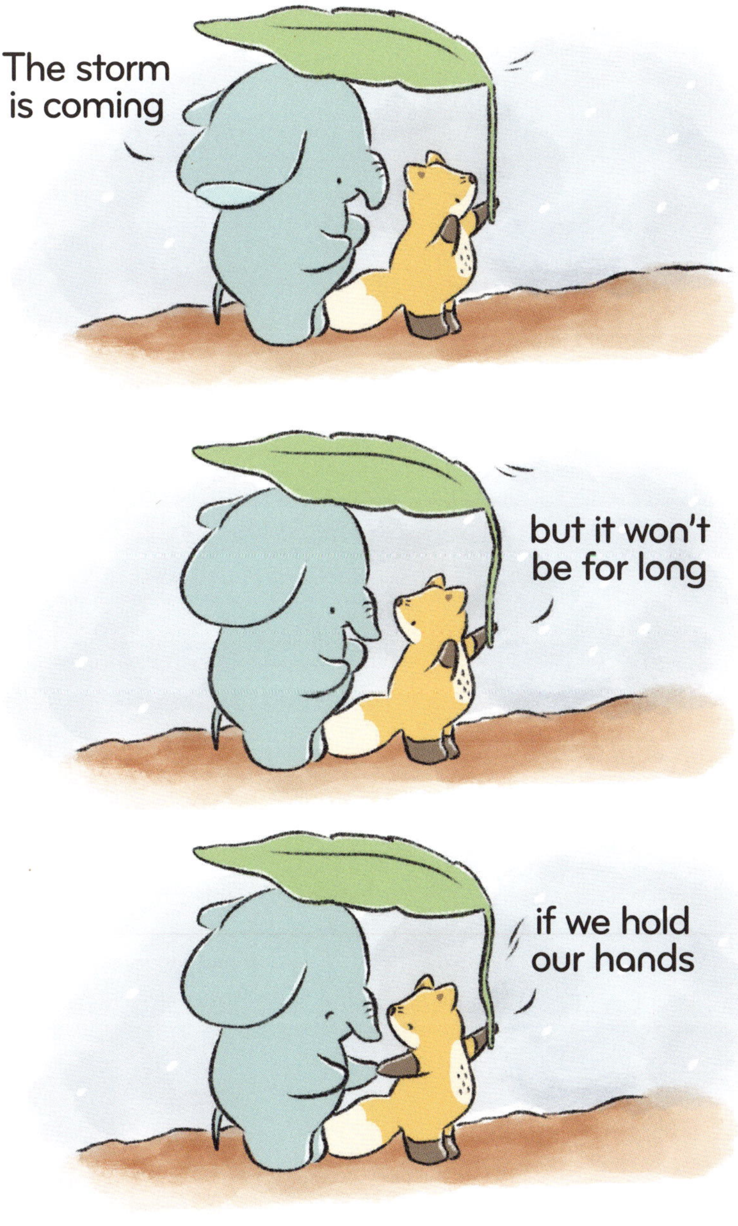
The storm is coming
but it won't be for long
if we hold our hands

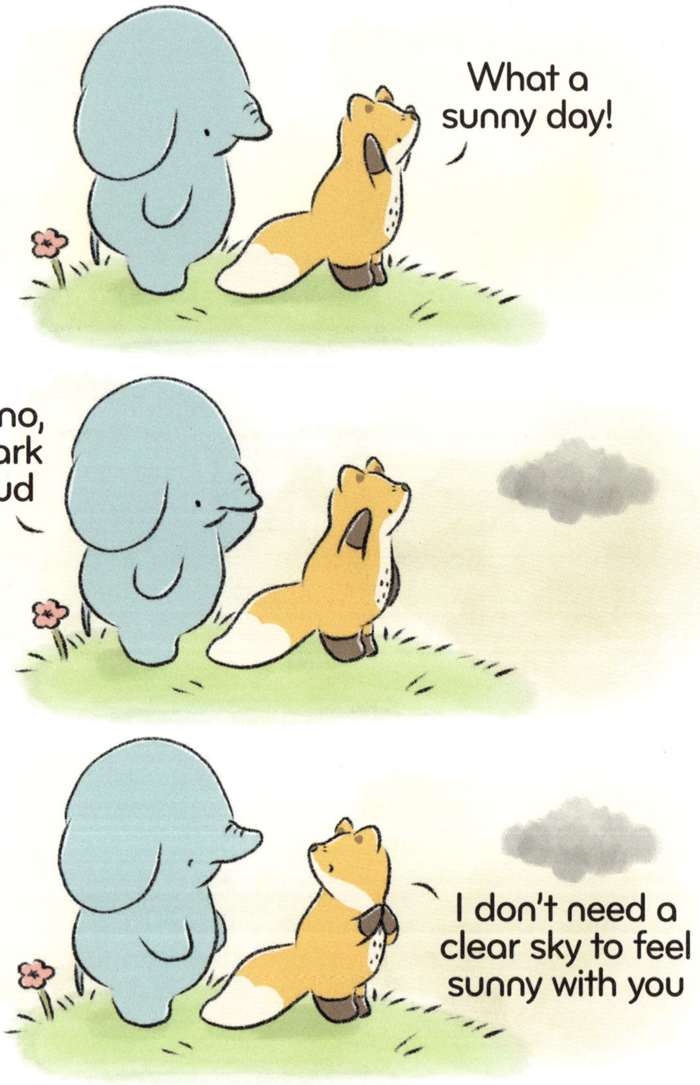
What a sunny day!
Oh no, a dark cloud
I don't need a clear sky to feel sunny with you

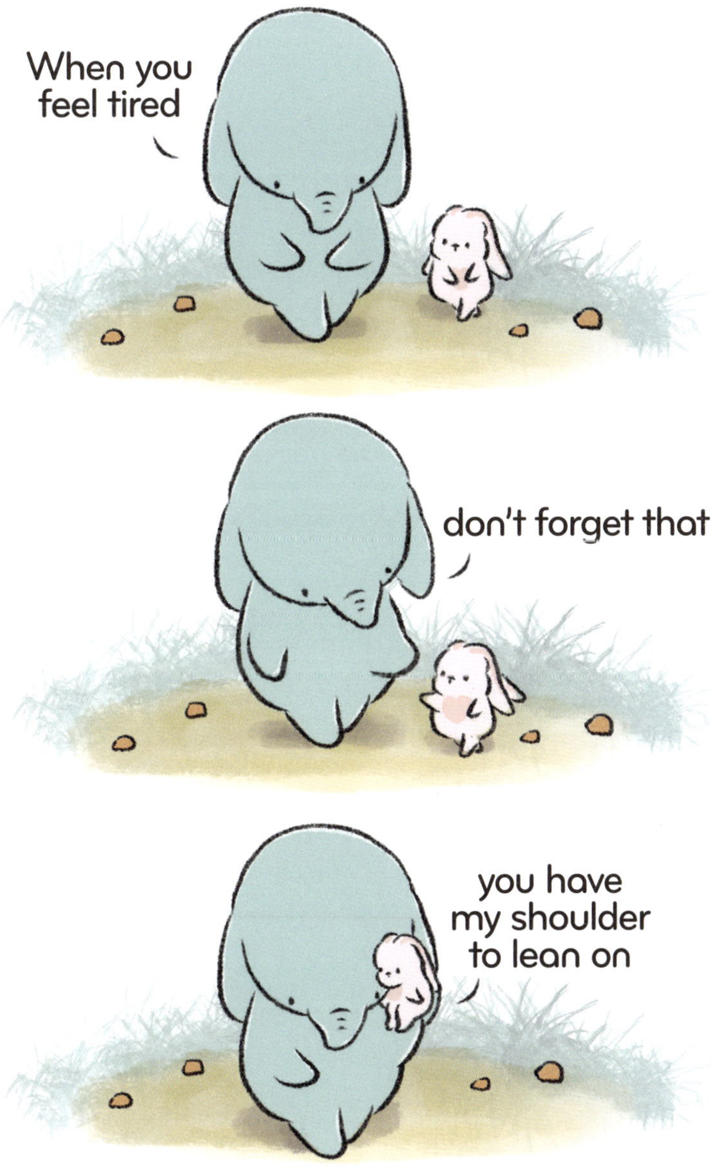
When you feel tired
don't forget that
you have my shoulder to lean on

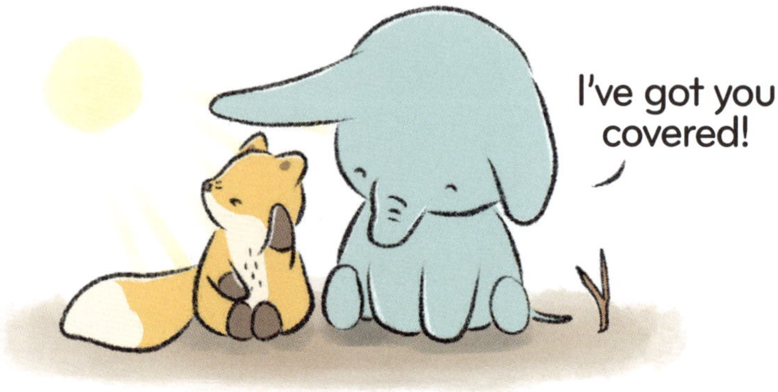
I've got you covered!

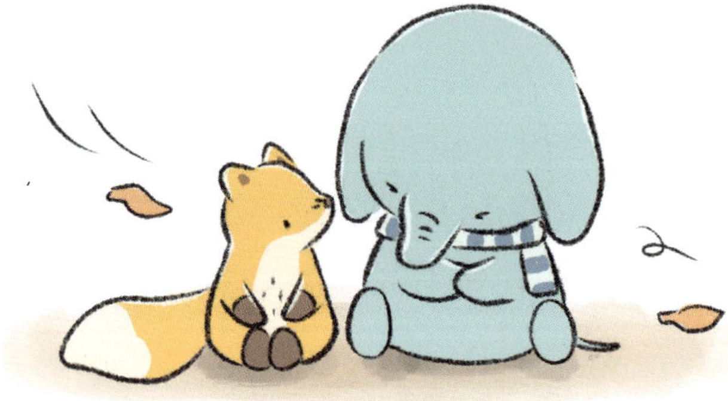

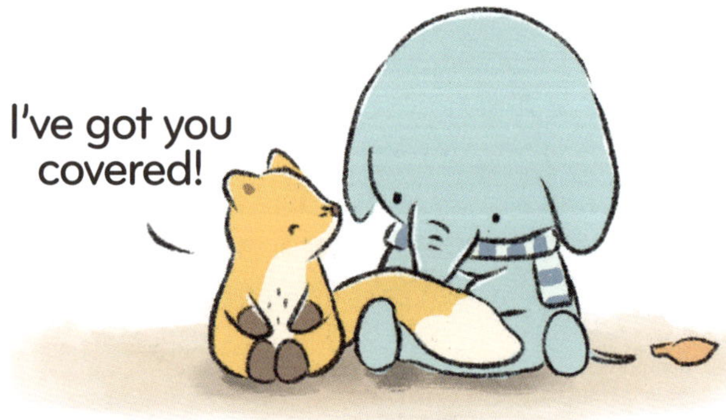
I've got you covered!

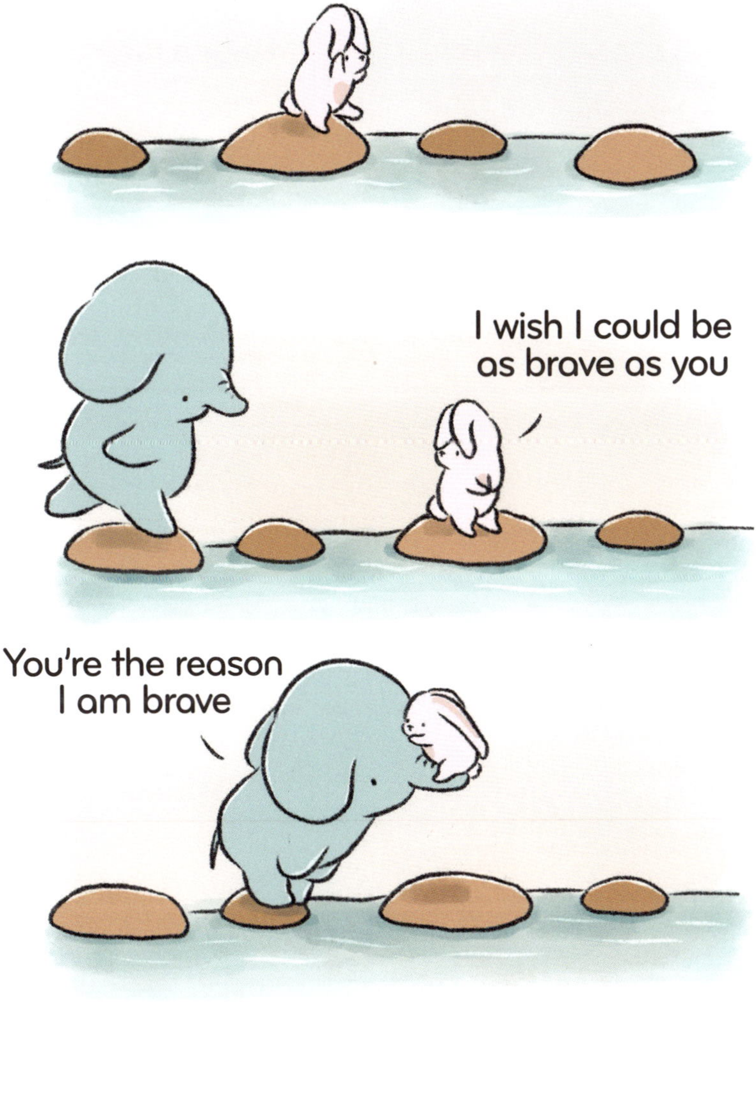
I wish I could be
as brave as you
You're the reason
I am brave

Emergency Pocket

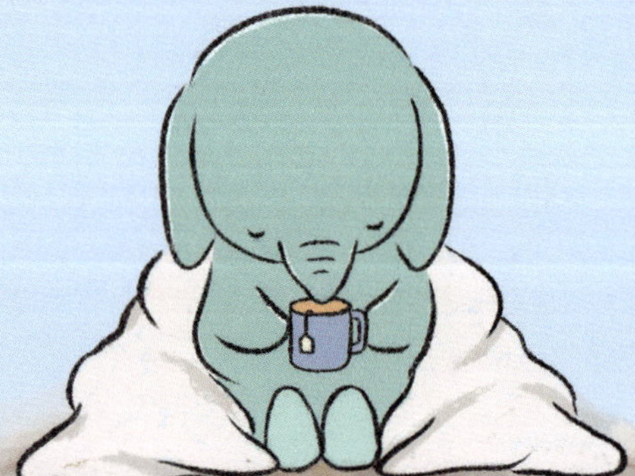

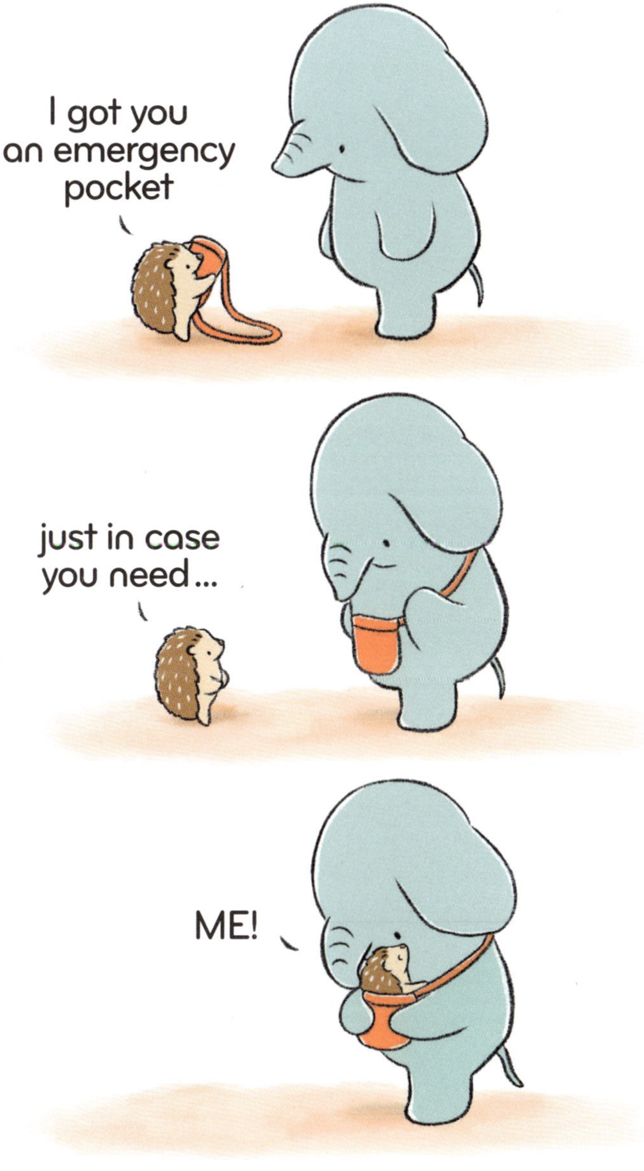
I got you an emergency pocket
just in case you need...
ME!

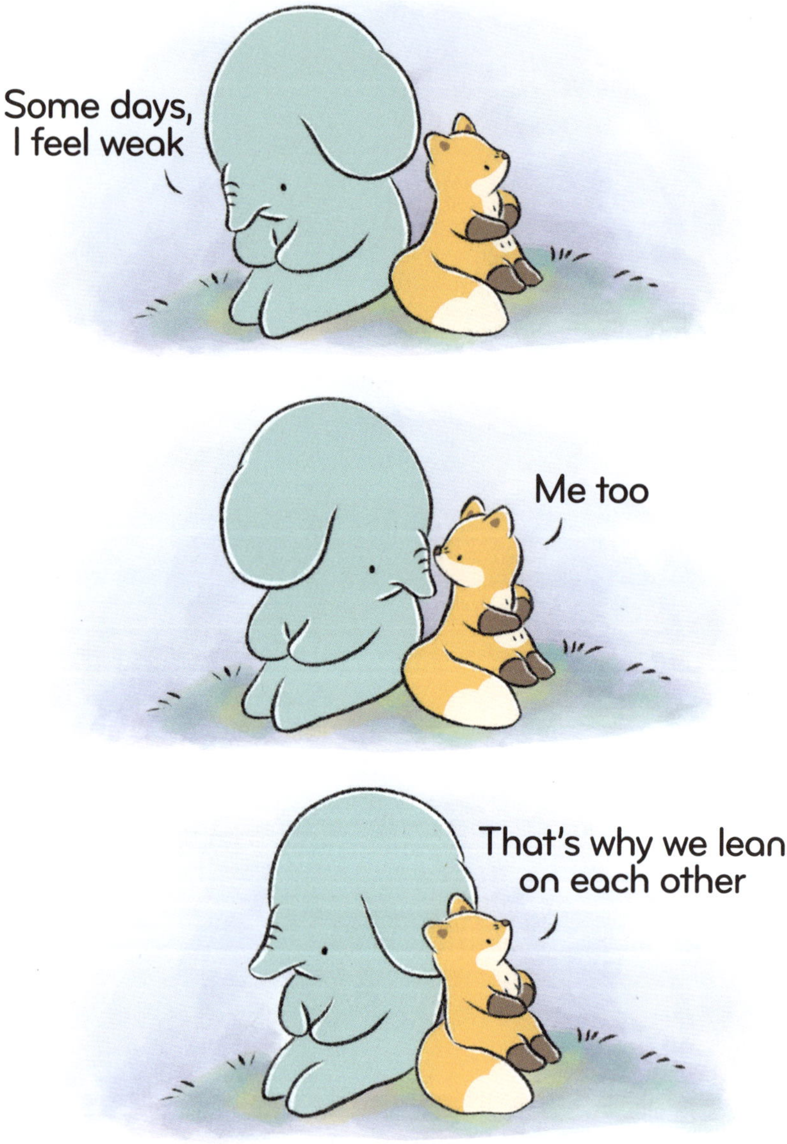
Some days,
I feel weak
Me too
That's why we lean
on each other

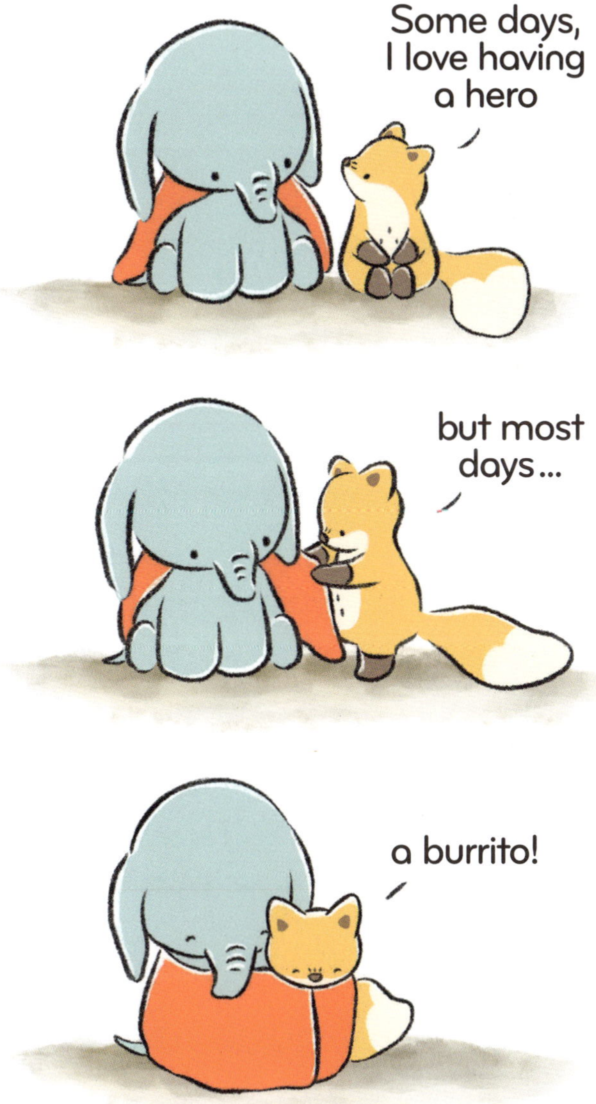
Some days, I love having a hero
but most days...
a burrito!

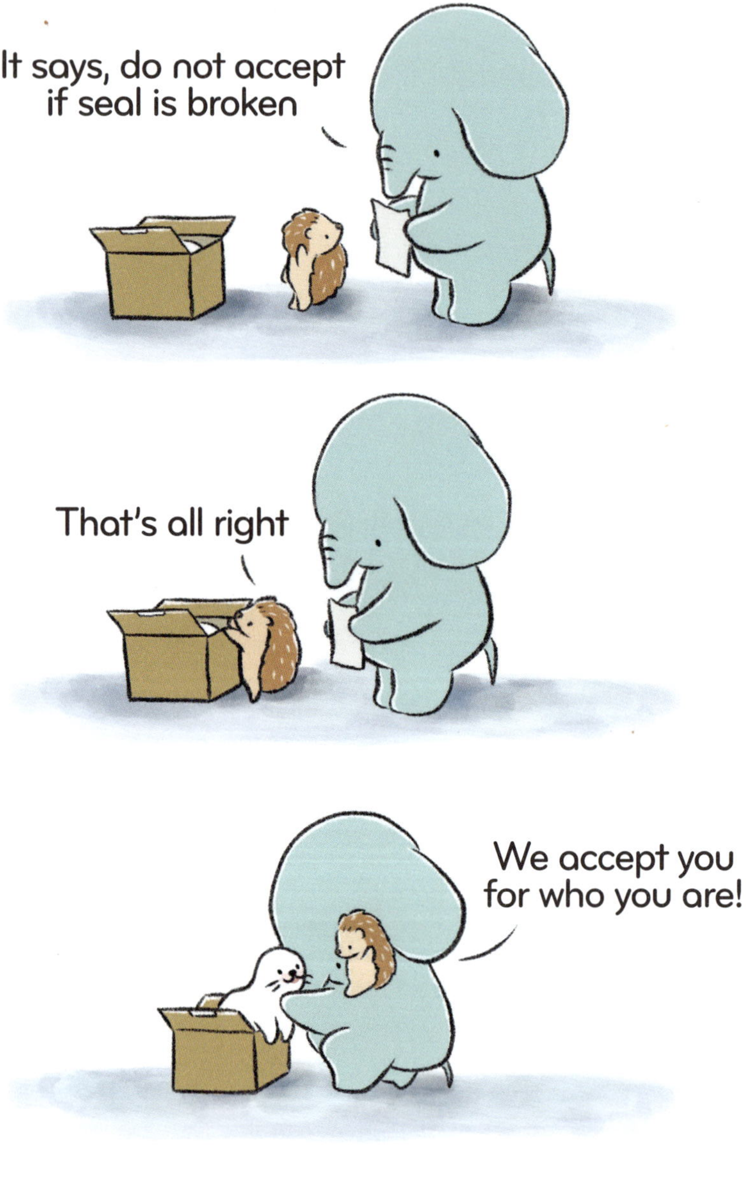
It says, do not accept if seal is broken
That's all right
We accept you for who you are!

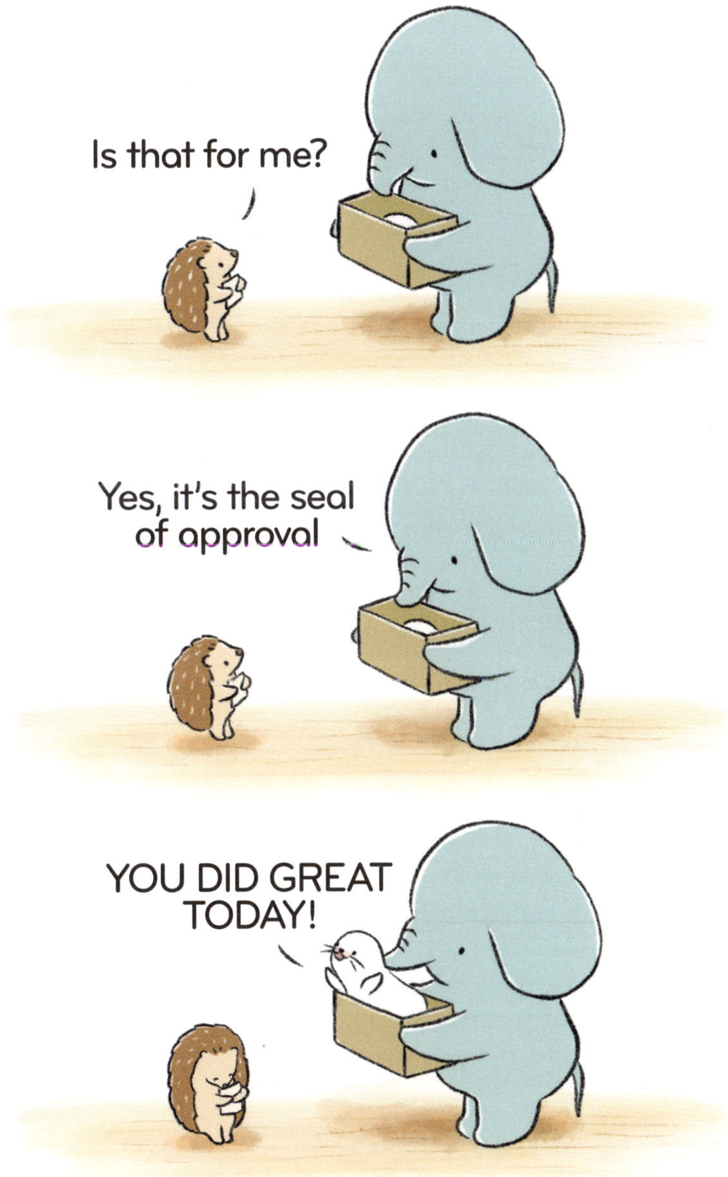
Is that for me?
Yes, it's the seal of approval
YOU DID GREAT TODAY!

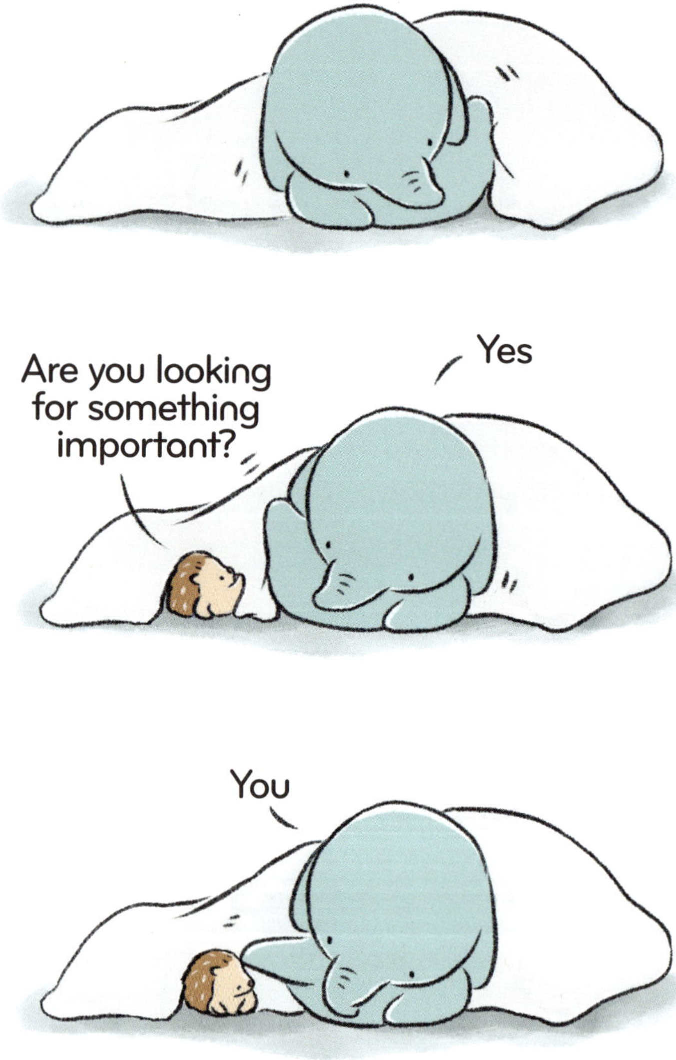
Are you looking for something important?
Yes
You

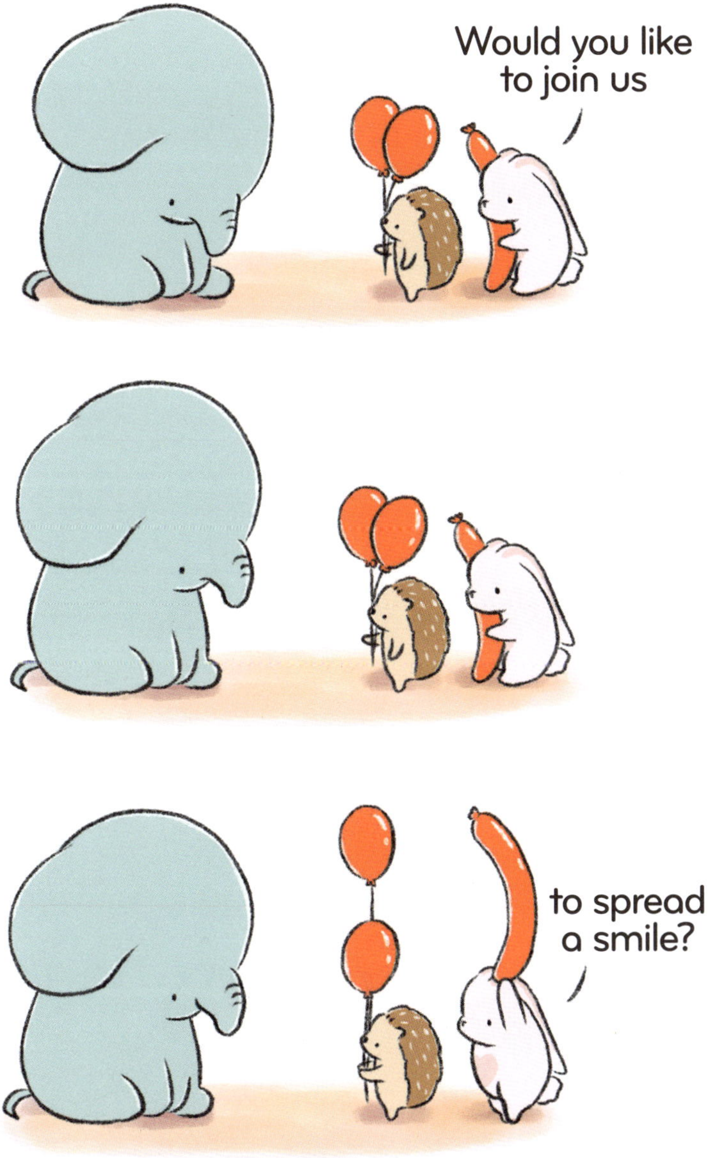
Would you like to join us
to spread a smile?

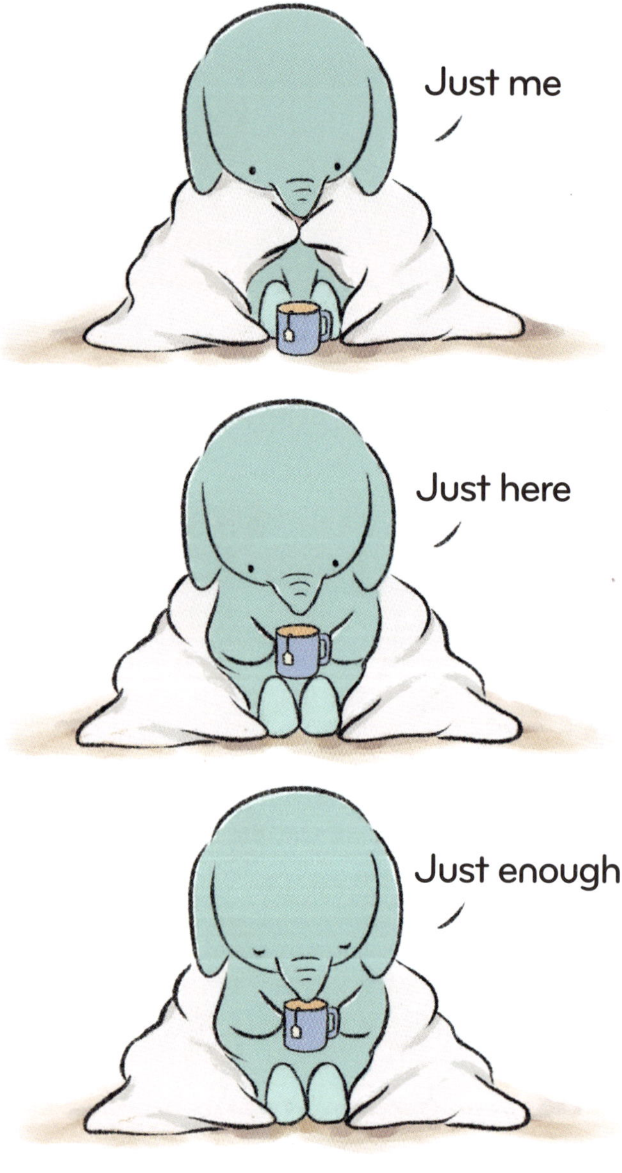
Just me
Just here
Just enough

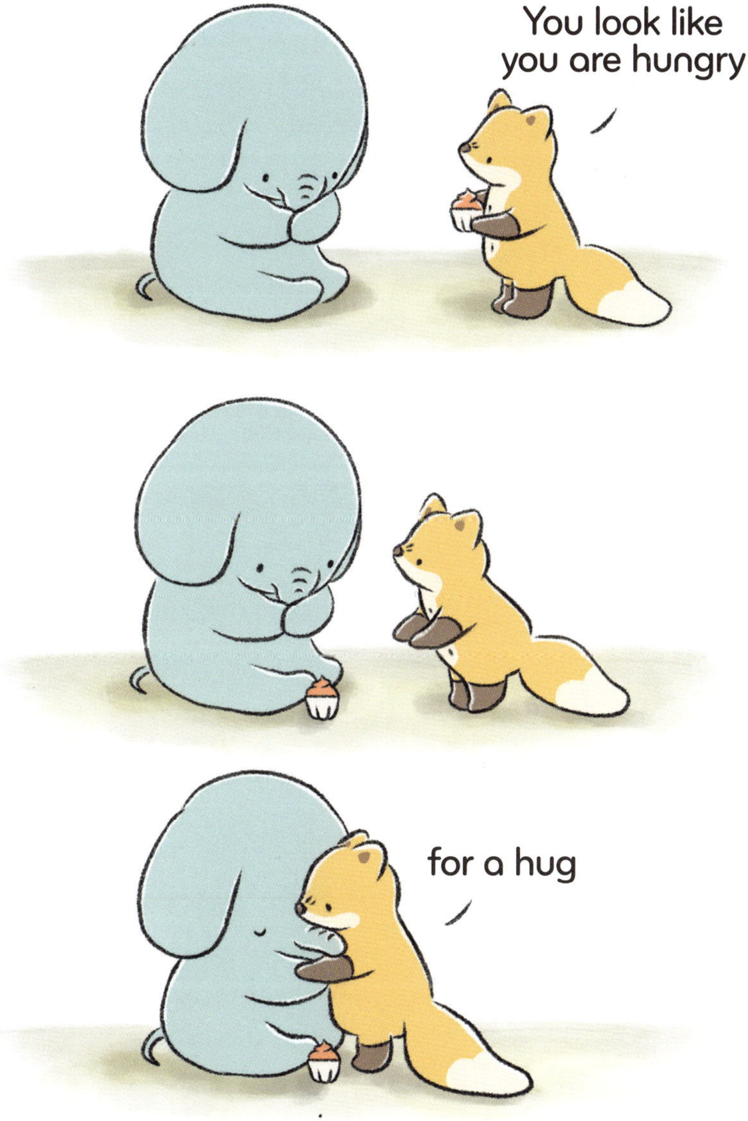
You look like
you are hungry
for a hug

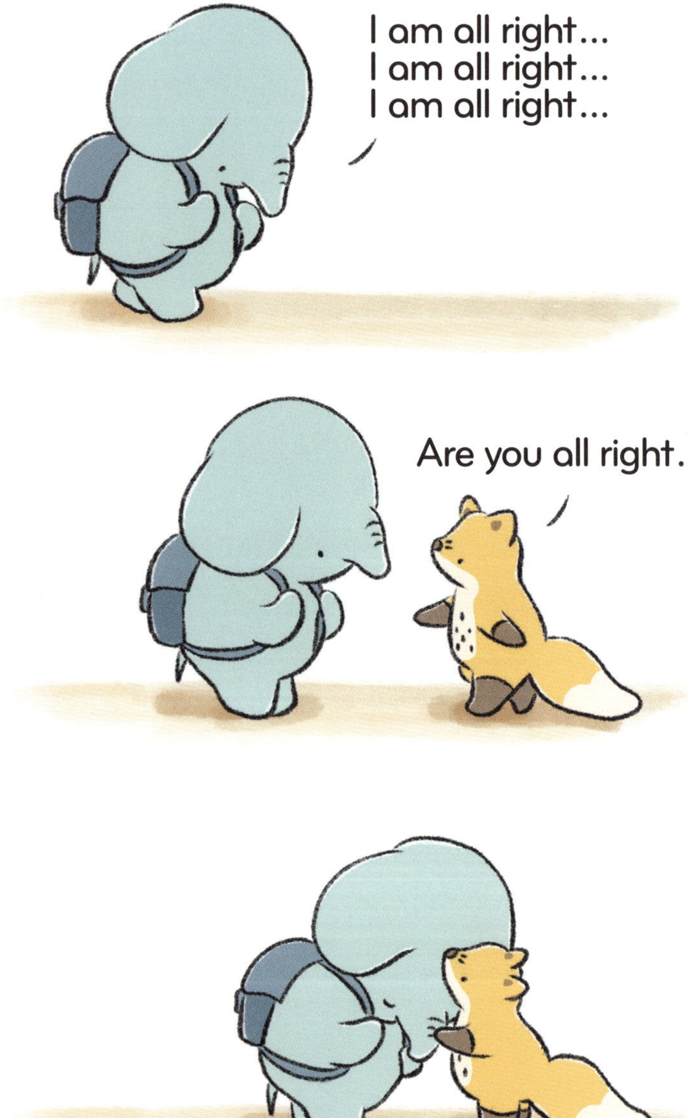
I am all right...
I am all right...
I am all right...
Are you all right...?

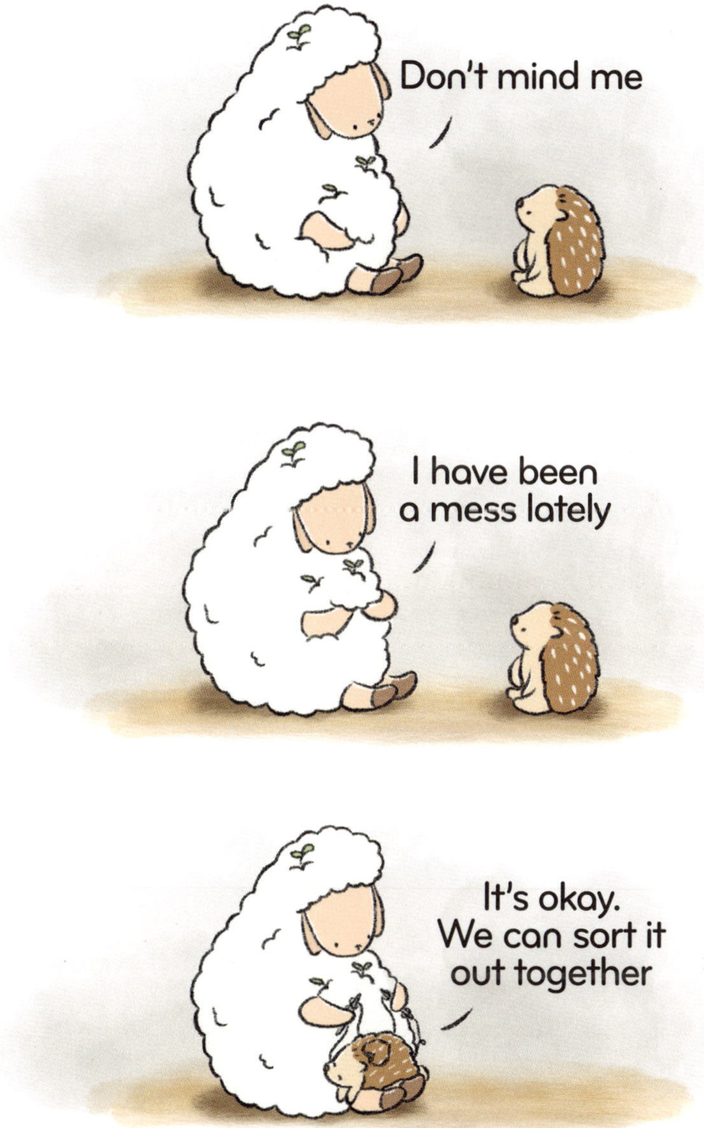
Don't mind me
I have been a mess lately
It's okay. We can sort it out together

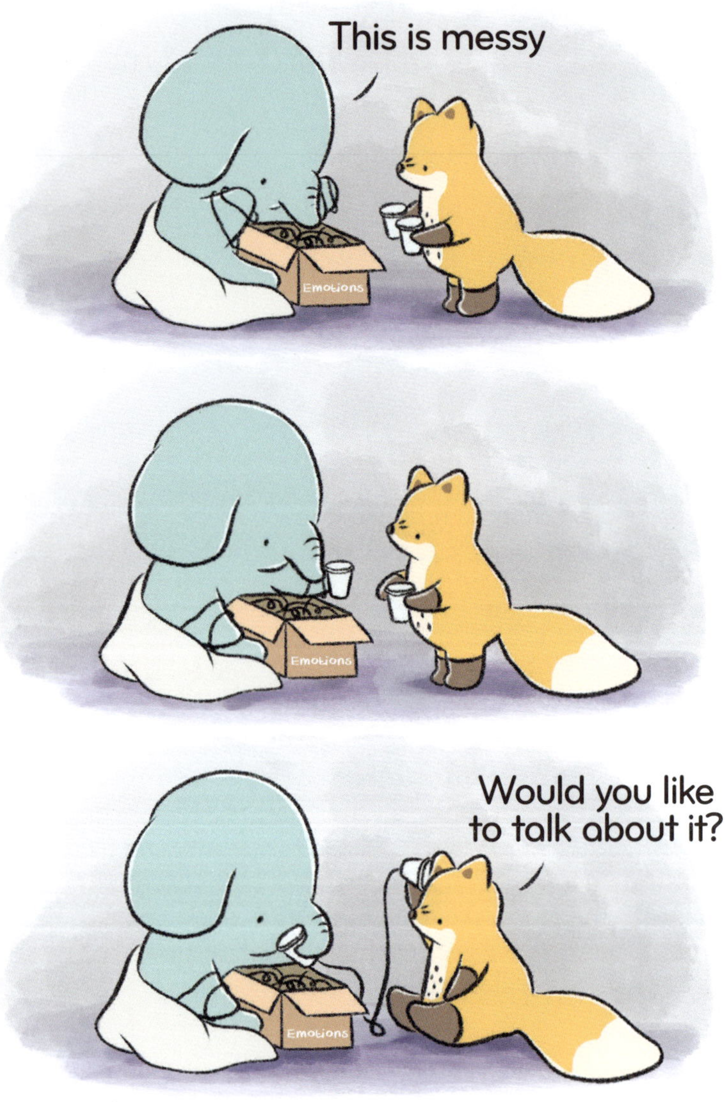
This is messy
Emotions
Emotions
Would you like to talk about it?
Emotions

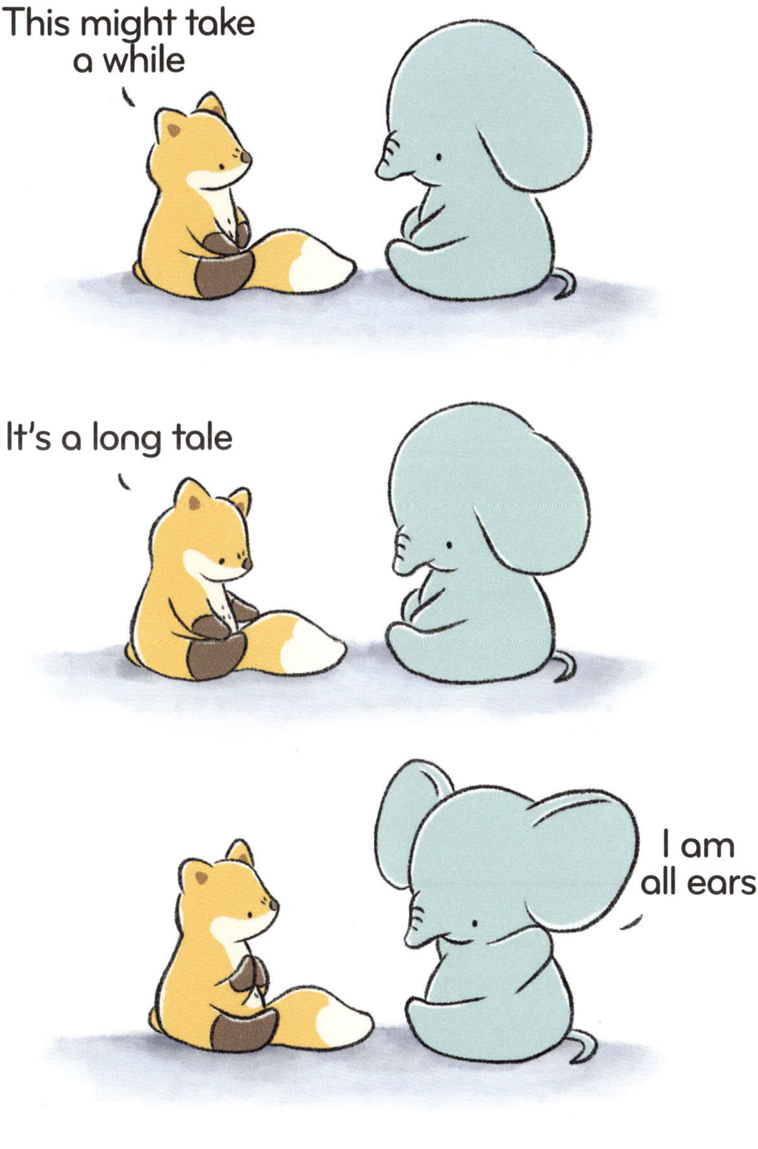
This might take a while
It's a long tale
I am all ears

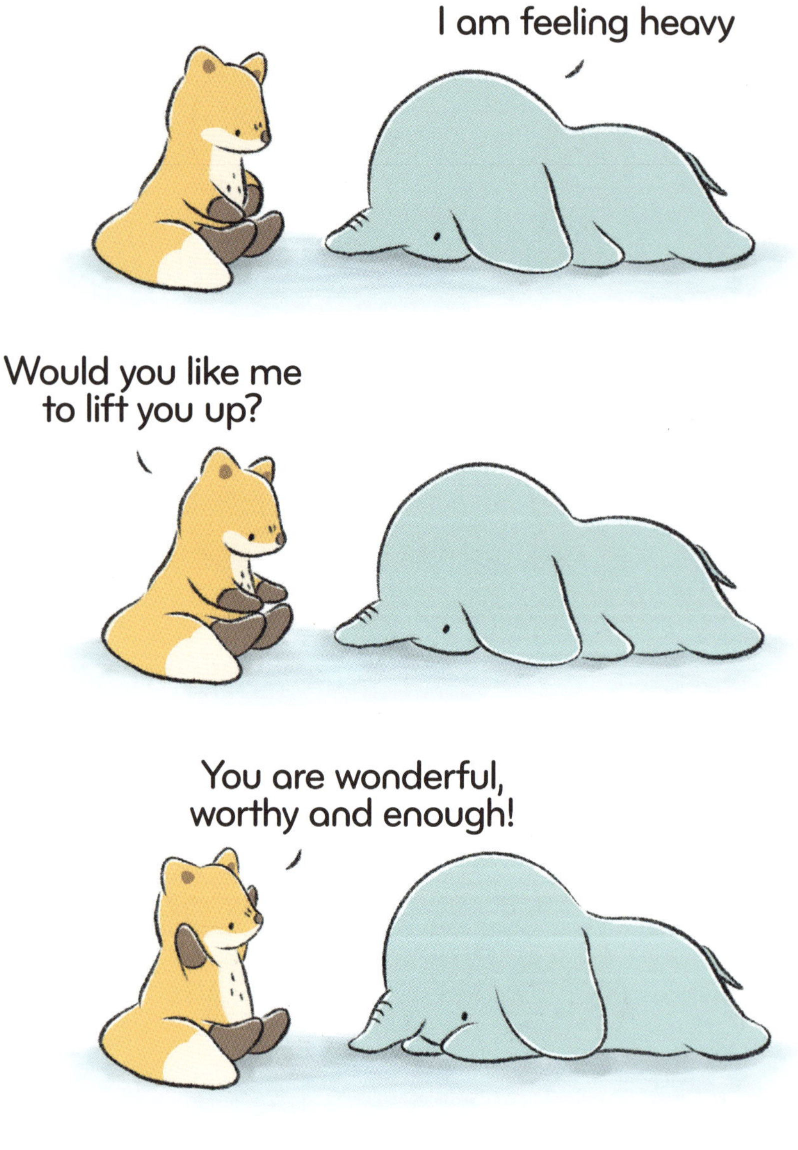
I am feeling heavy
Would you like me to lift you up?
You are wonderful, worthy and enough!

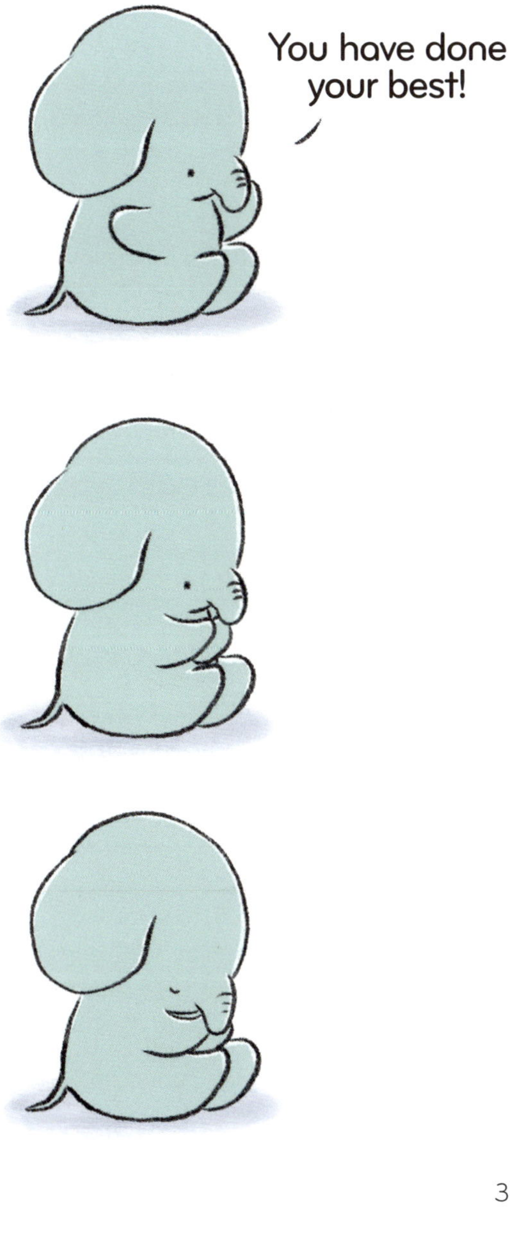
You have done your best!

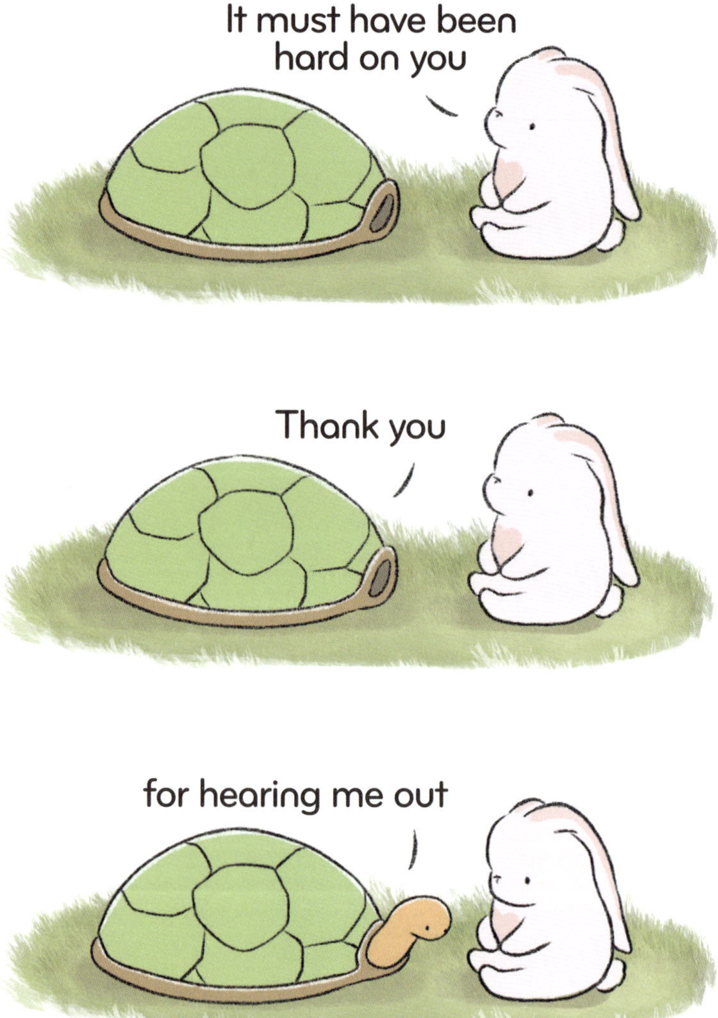
It must have been hard on you
Thank you
for hearing me out

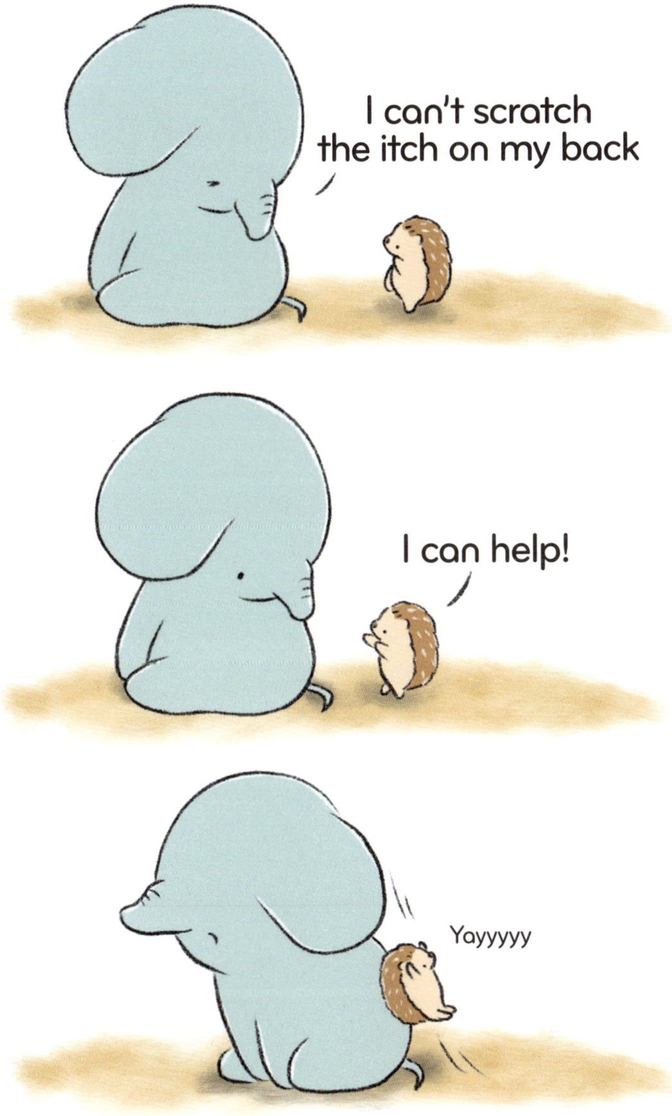
I can't scratch the itch on my back
I can help!
Yayyyyy

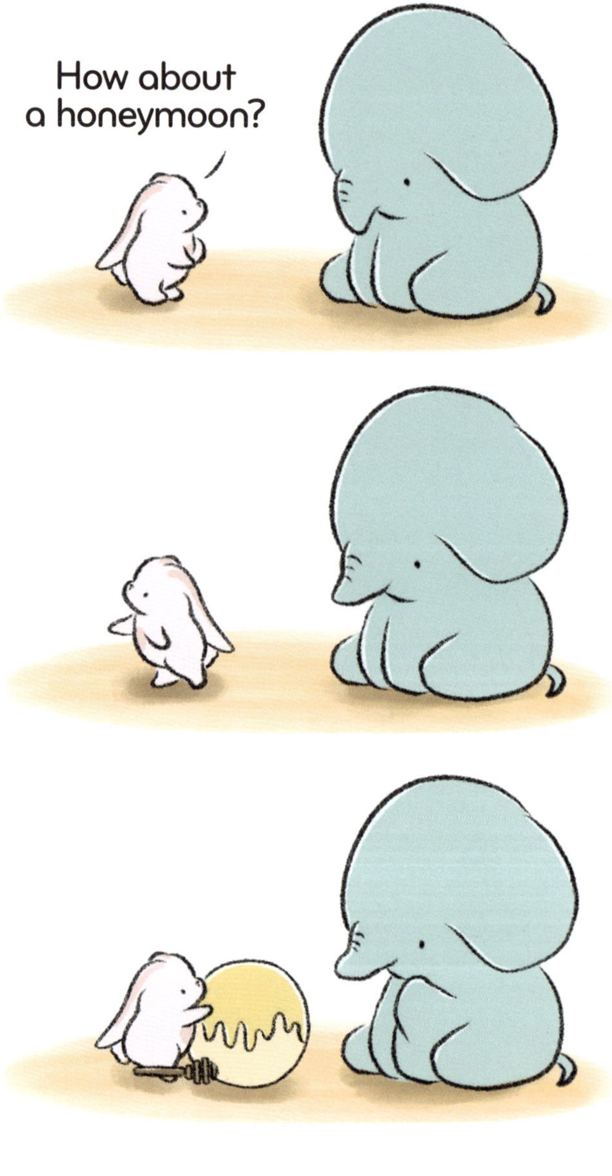
How about
a honeymoon?

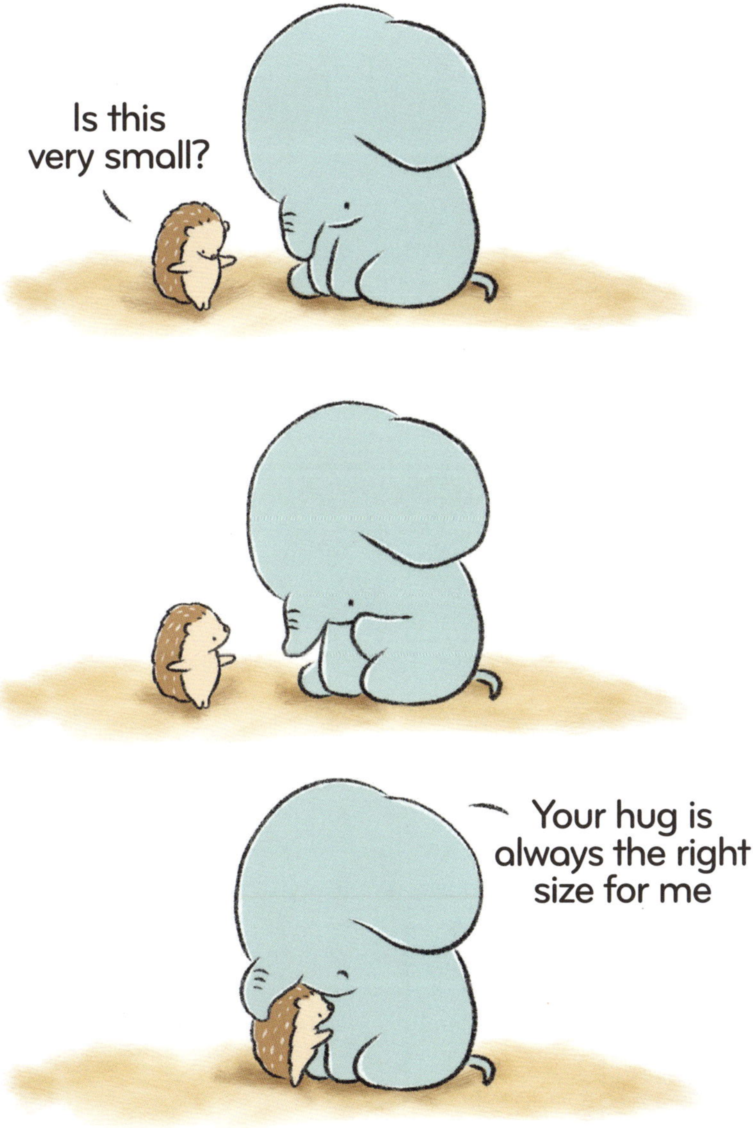
Is this very small?
Your hug is always the right size for me

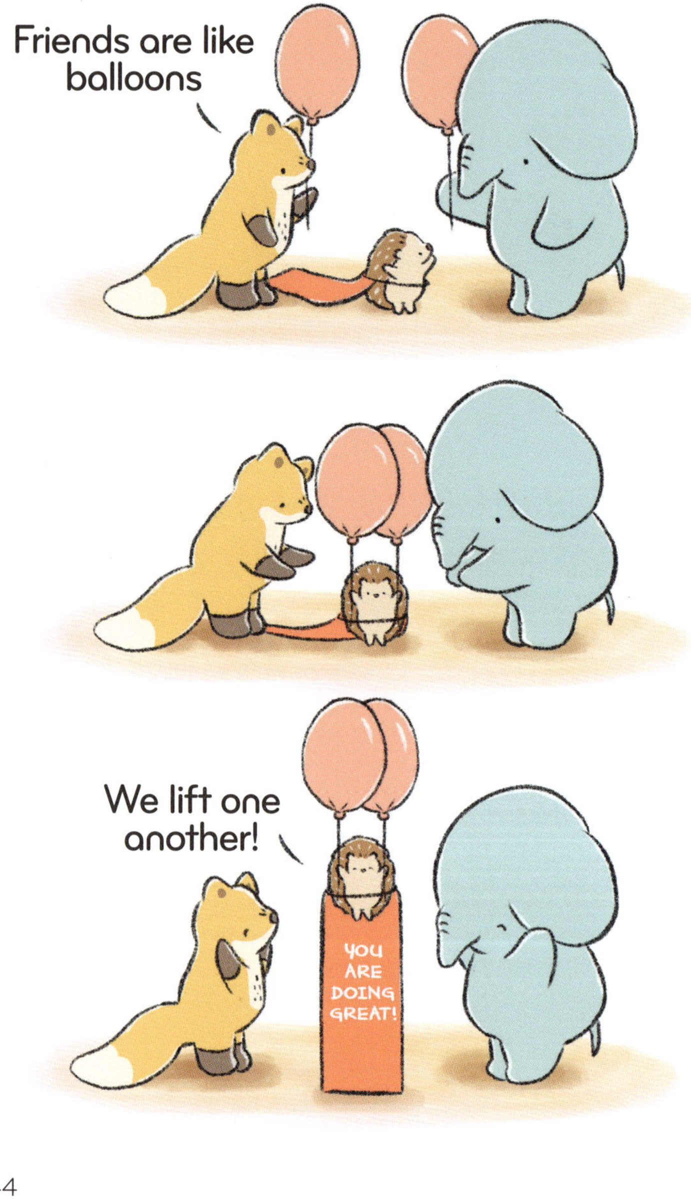
Friends are like balloons
We lift one another!
YOU ARE DOING GREAT!

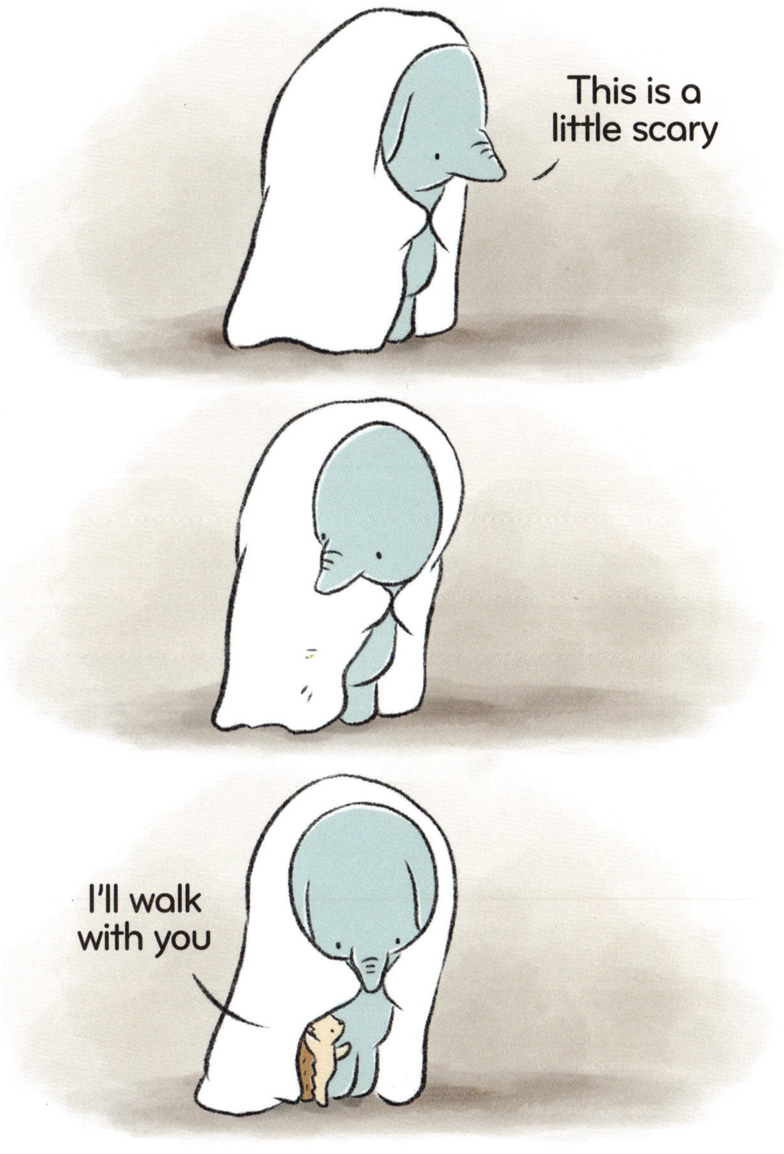
This is a little scary
I'll walk with you

Little Steps

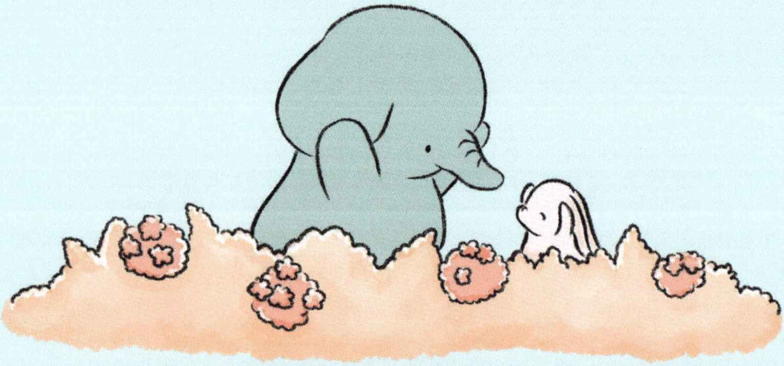

Some days, we take giant steps

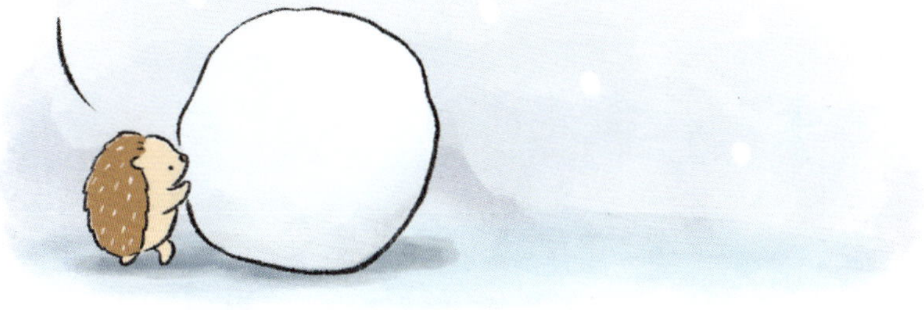

Some days, we inch little by little

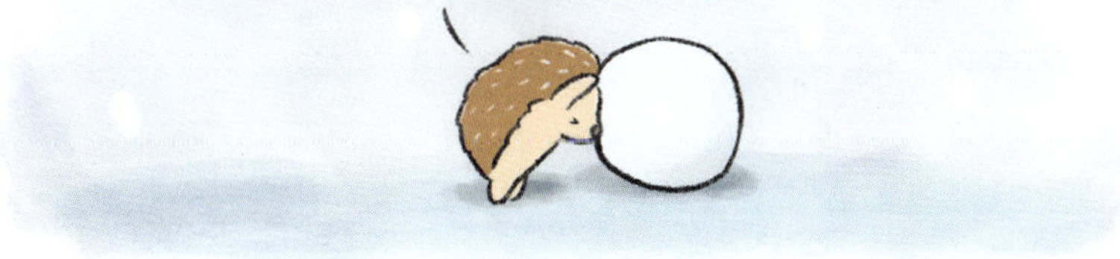

Both are necessary
and okay

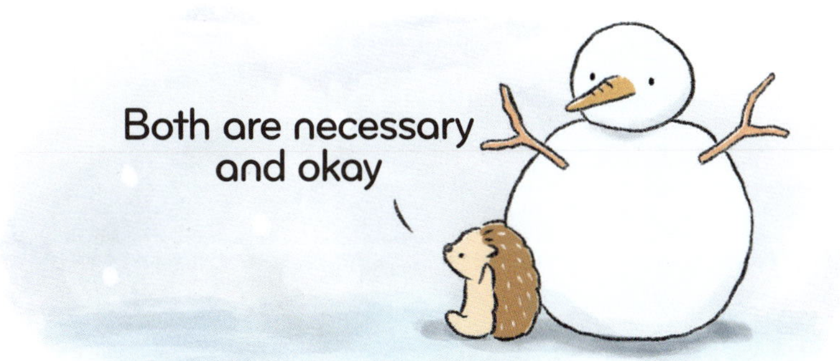

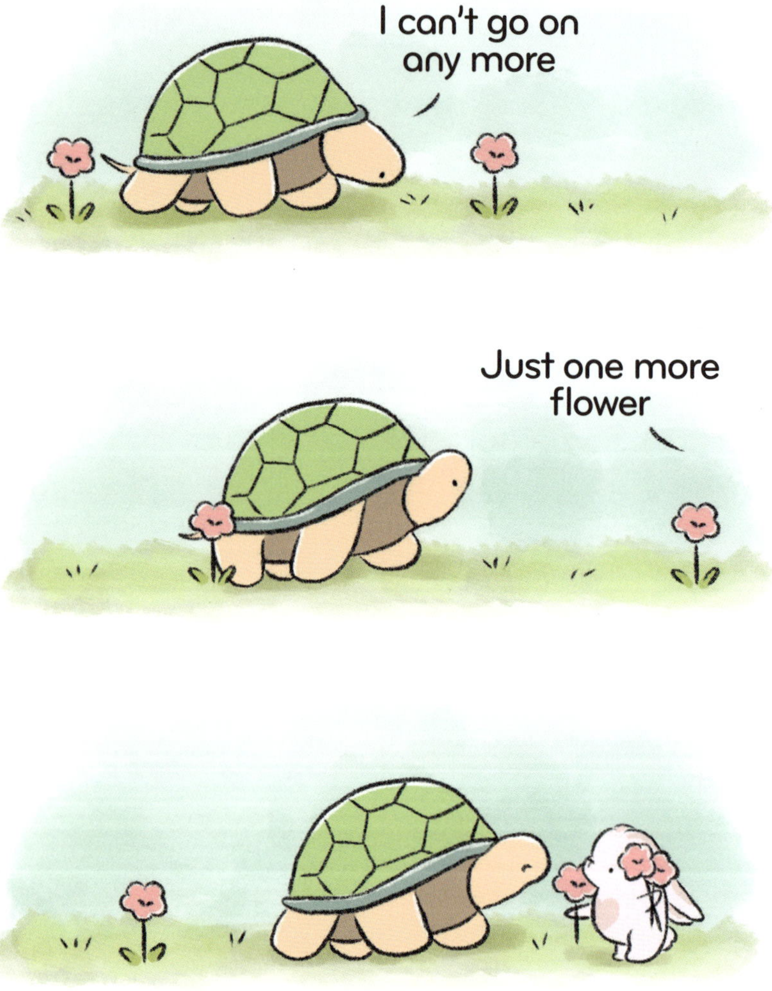
I can't go on any more
Just one more flower

Things will get bitter

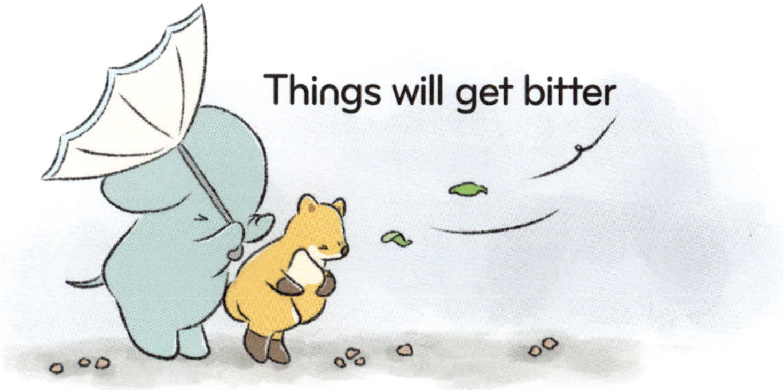

And little by little

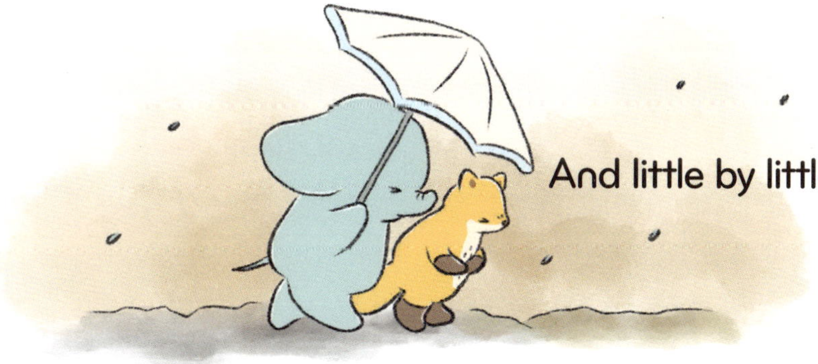

things will get better

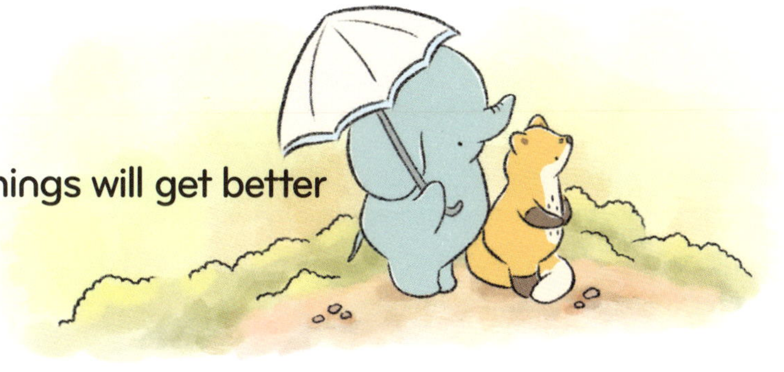

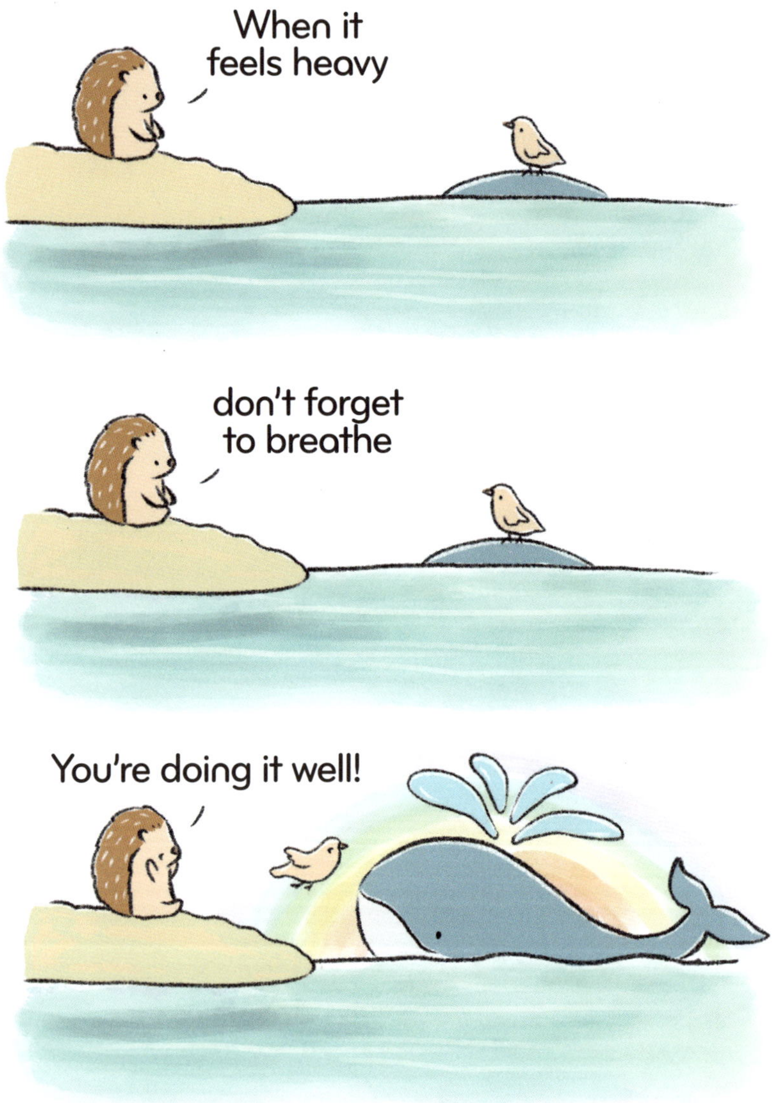
When it
feels heavy
don't forget
to breathe
You're doing it well!

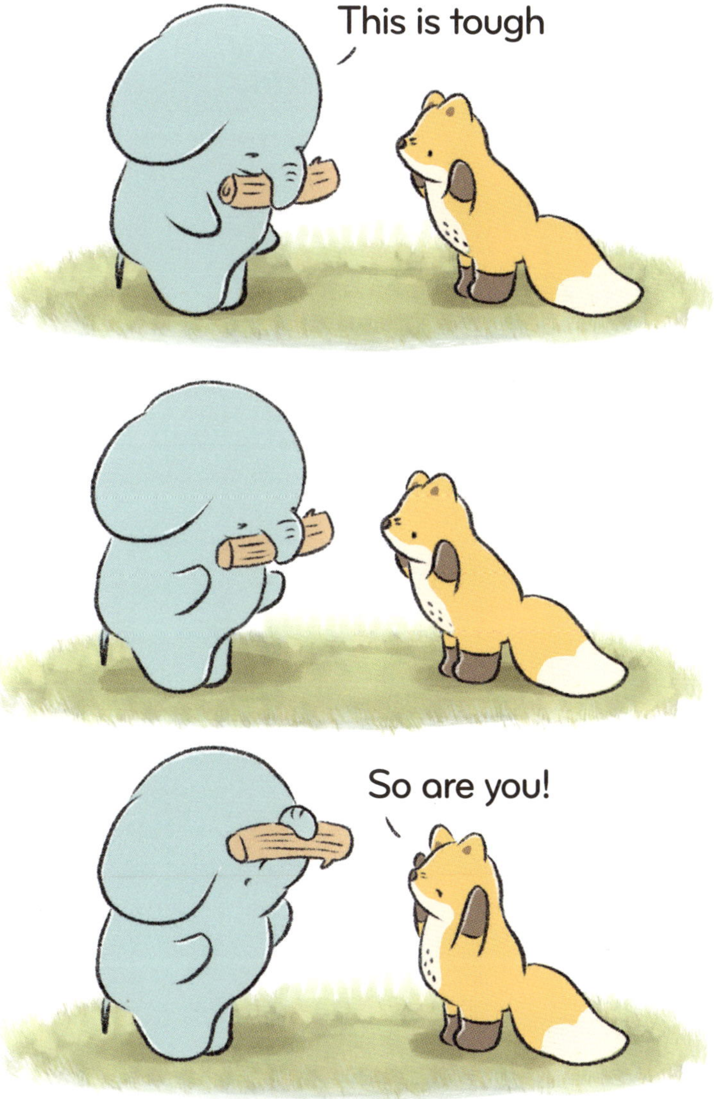
This is tough
So are you!

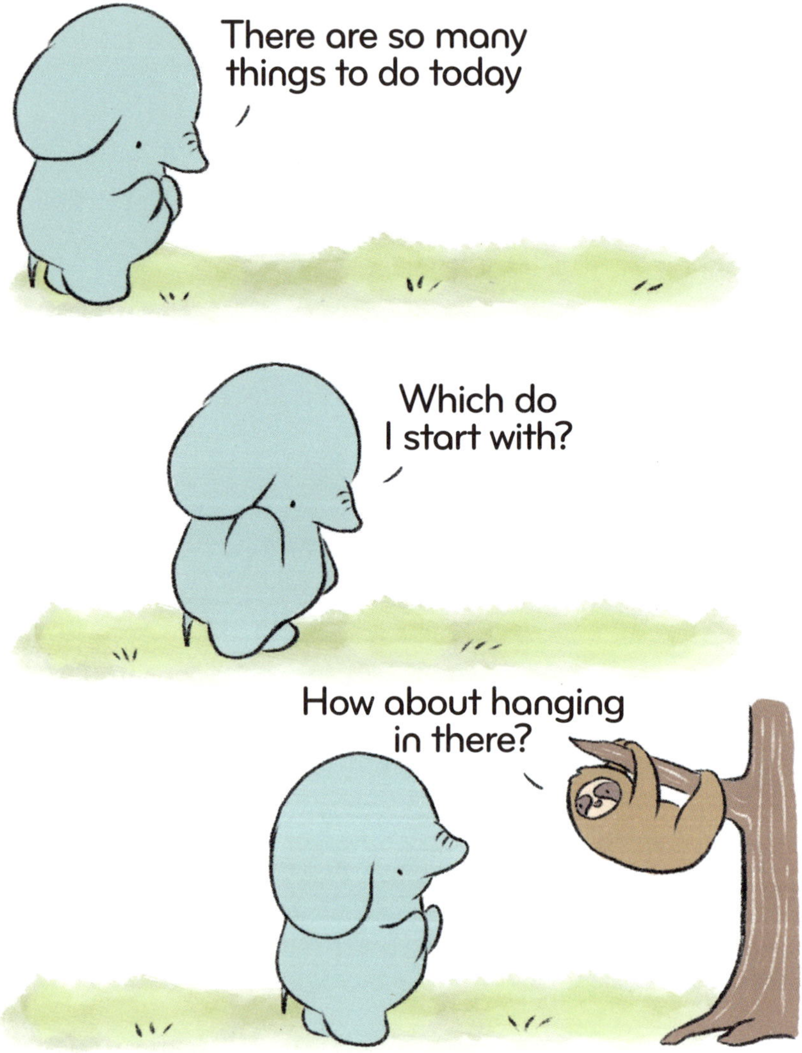
There are so many things to do today
Which do I start with?
How about hanging in there?

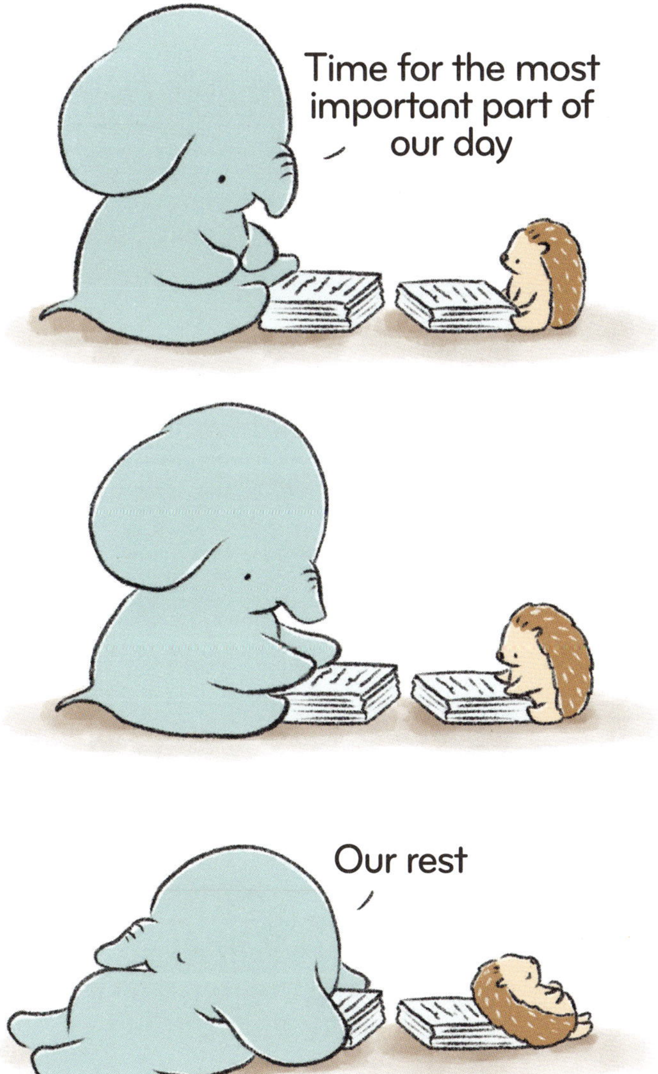
Time for the most important part of our day
Our rest

If you find yourself in a dark place,

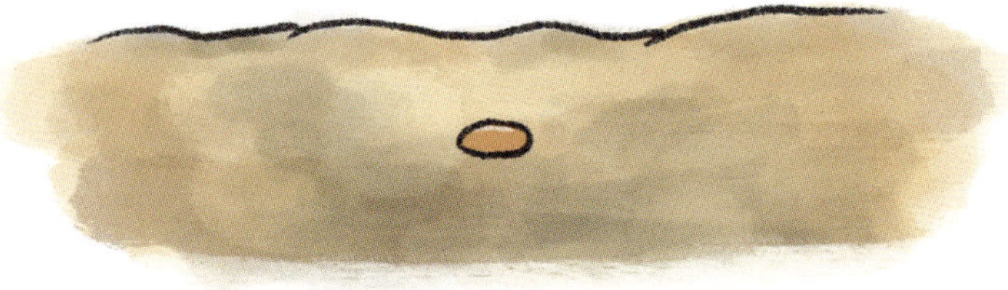

trust that you are not forgotten

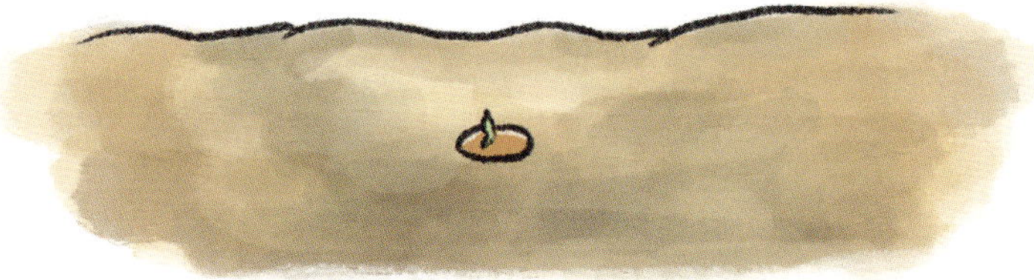

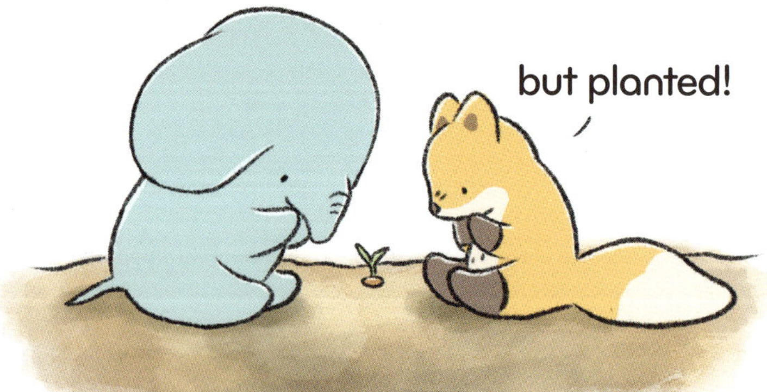

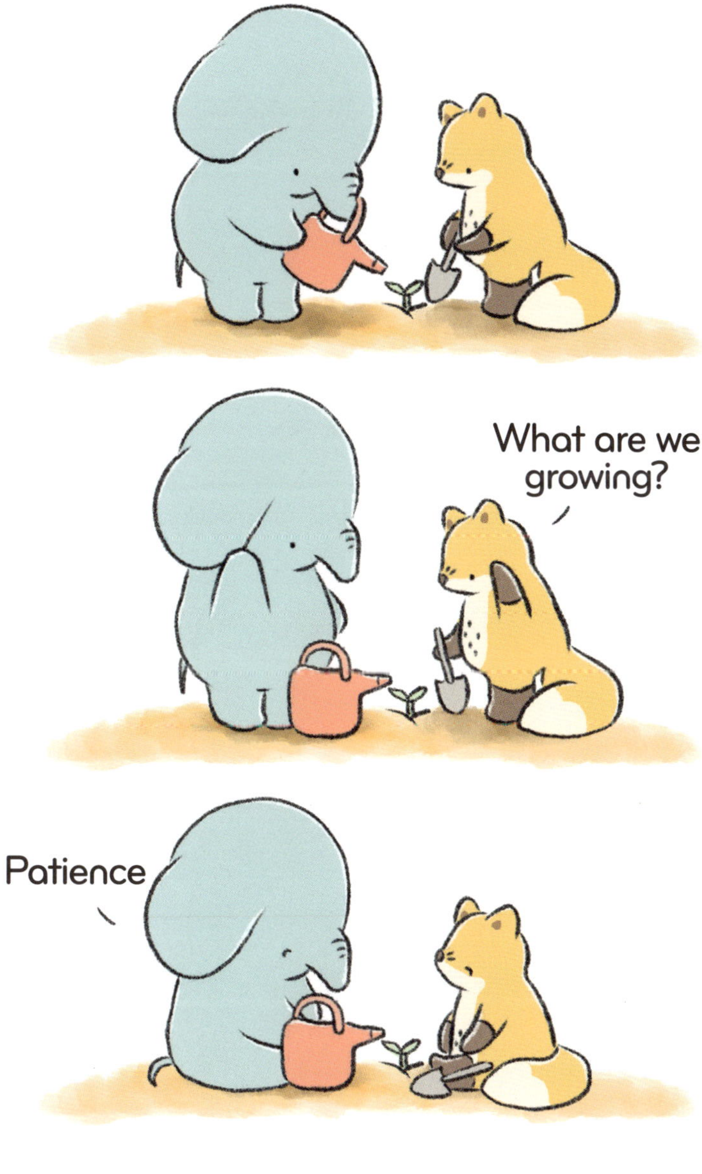
What are we growing?
Patience

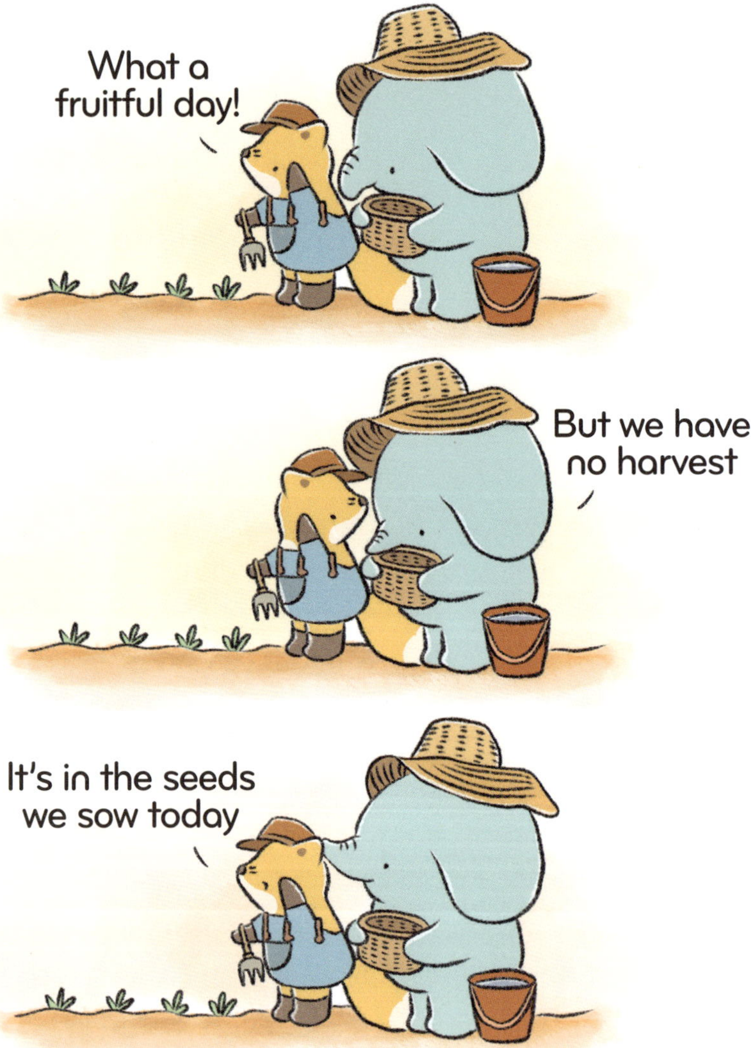
What a fruitful day!
But we have no harvest
It's in the seeds we sow today

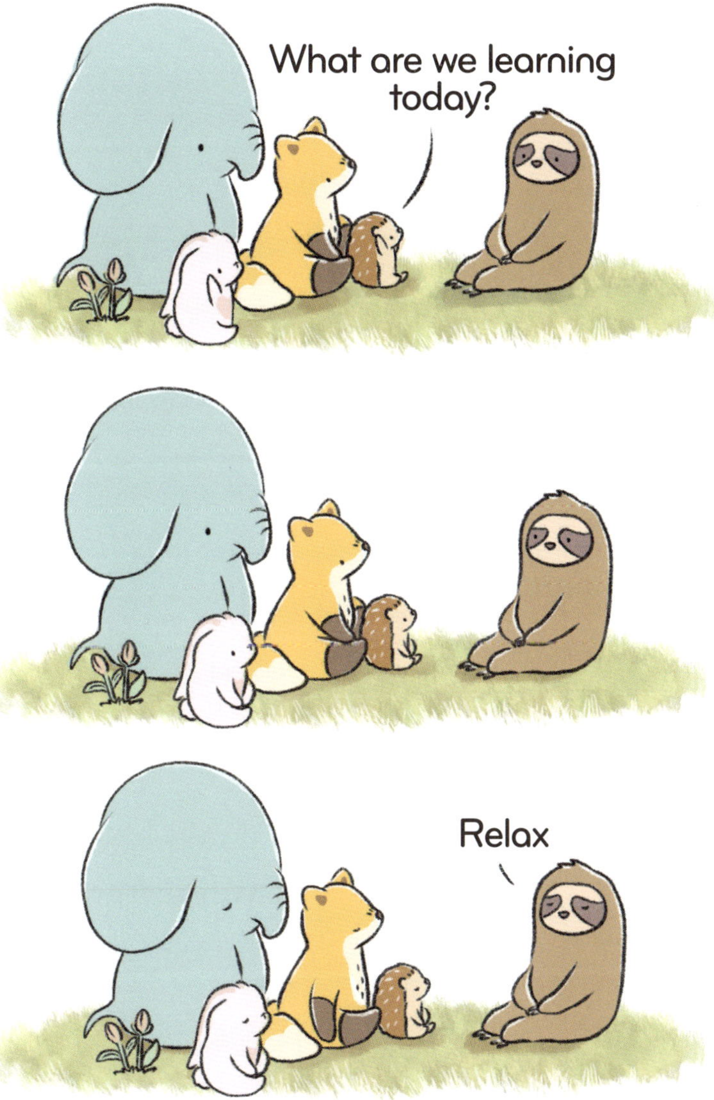
What are we learning today?
Relax

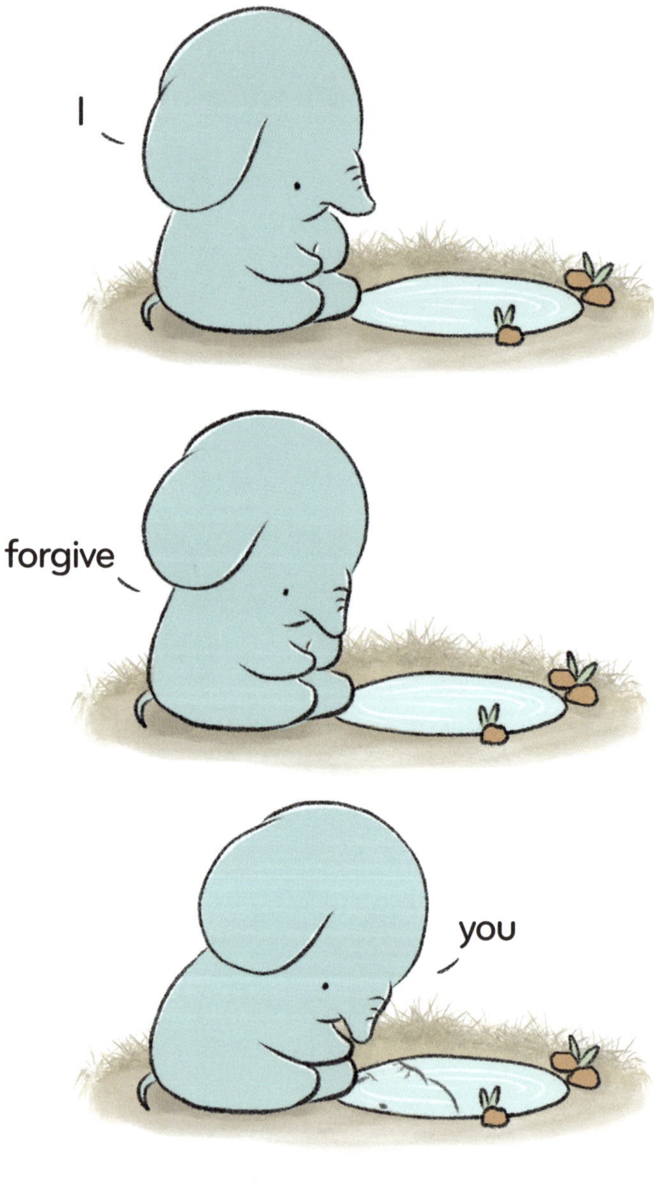
I
forgive
you

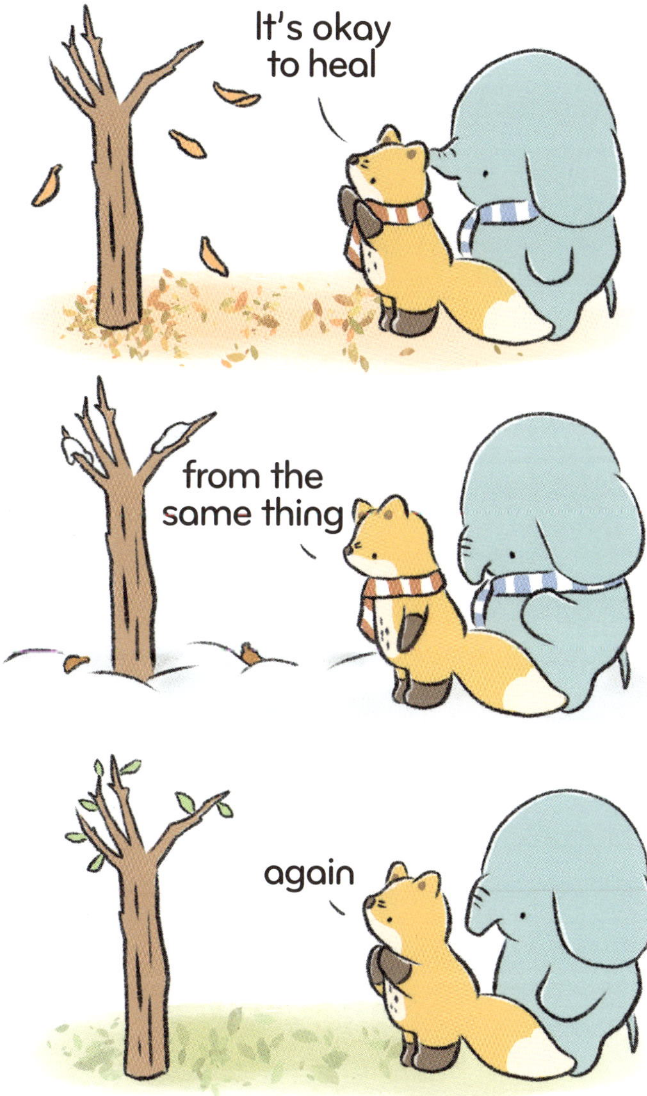
It's okay
to heal
from the
same thing
again

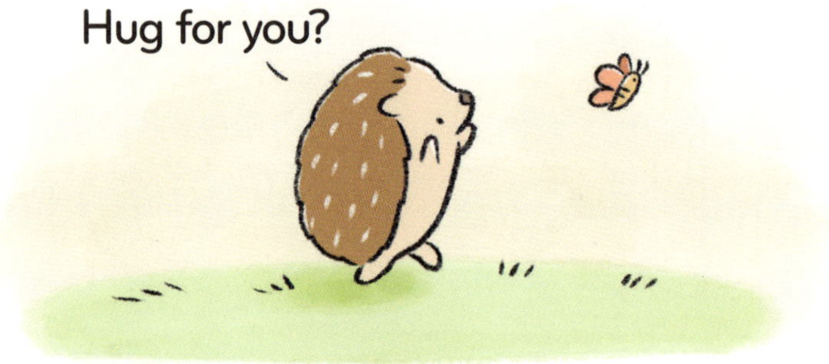
Hug for you?

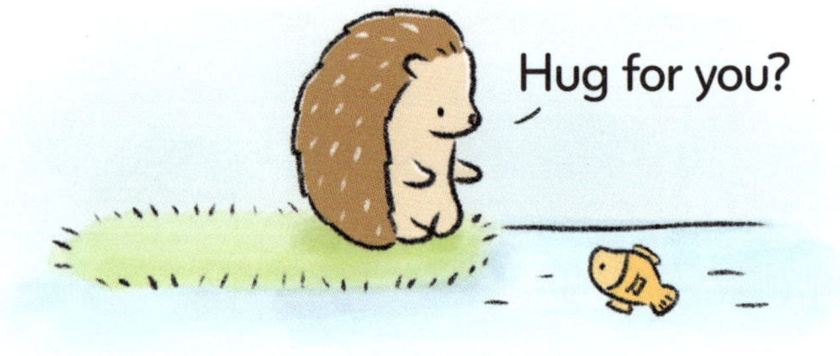
Hug for you?

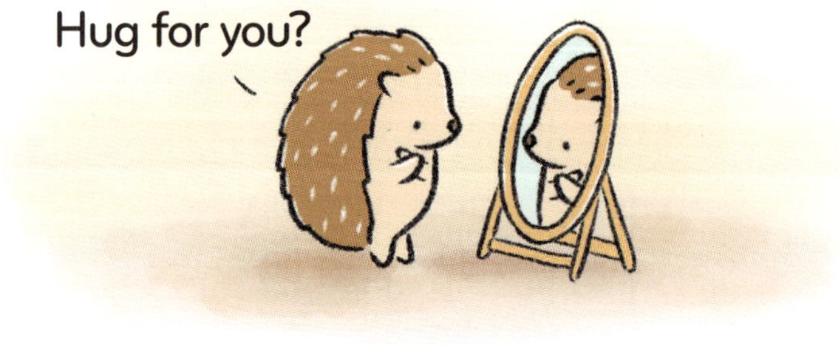
Hug for you?

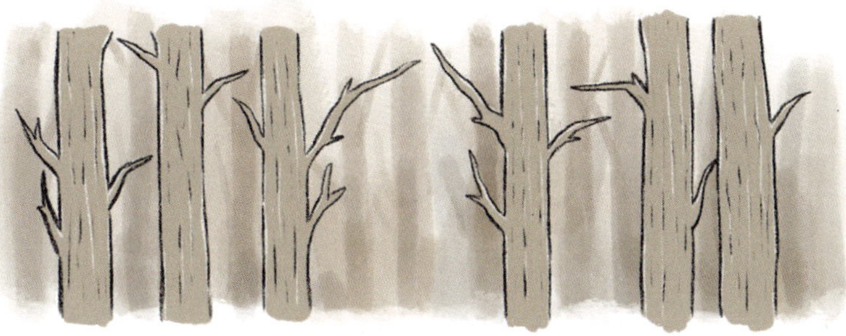

Even in the thickest forest

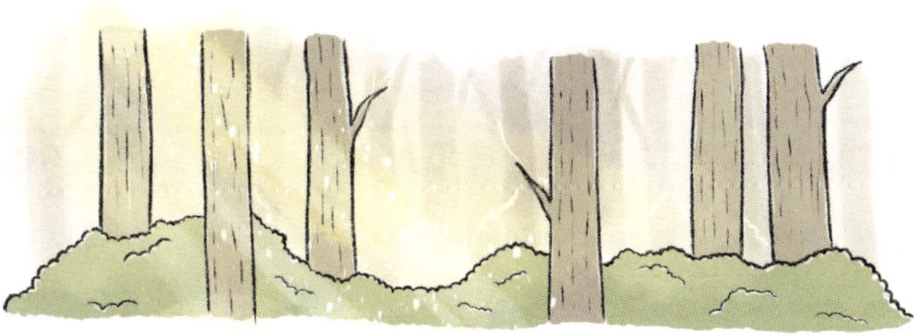

the light

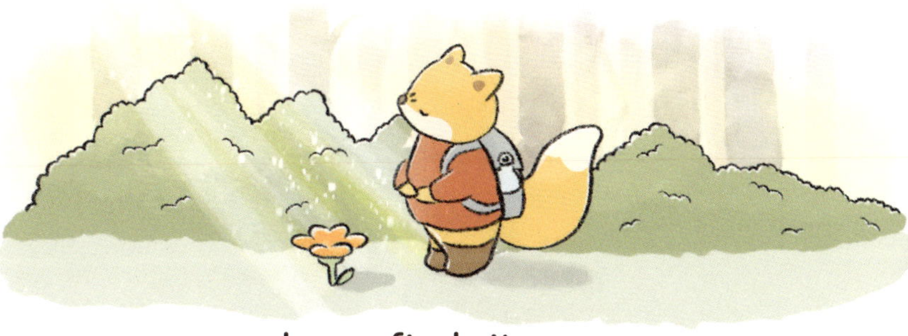

always finds its way

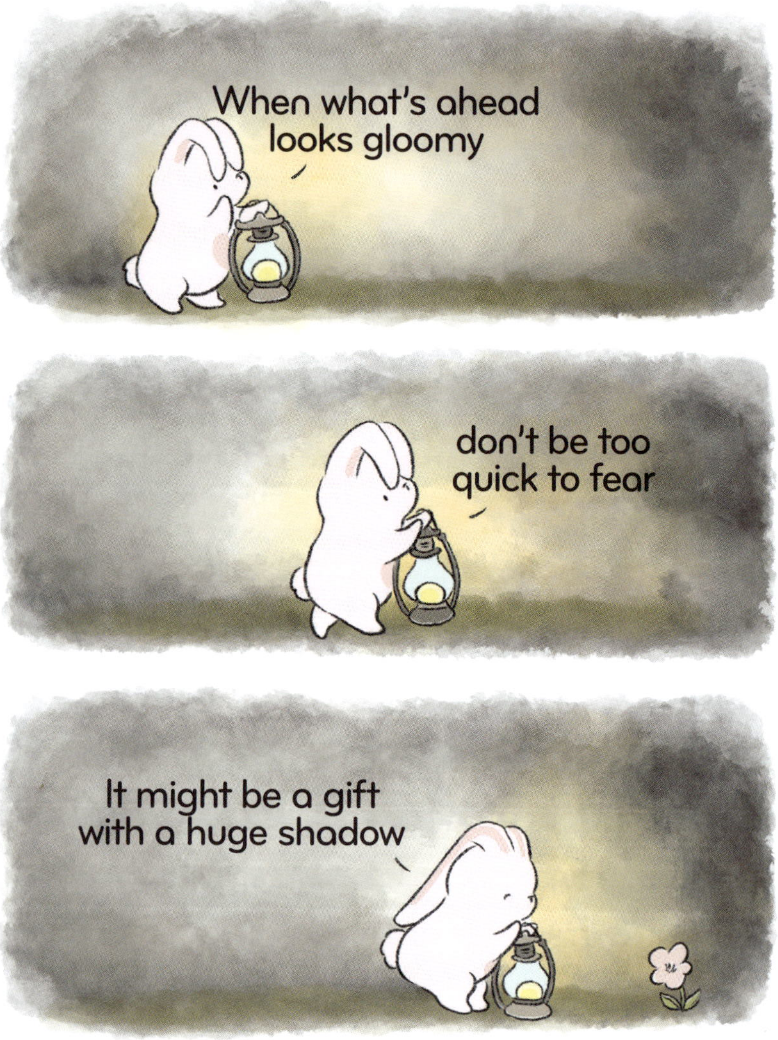
When what's ahead looks gloomy
don't be too quick to fear
It might be a gift with a huge shadow

When the journey looks winding and scary

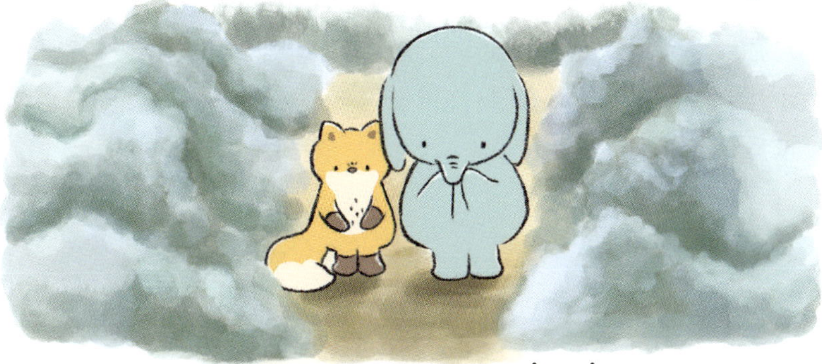

we can conquer our shadow

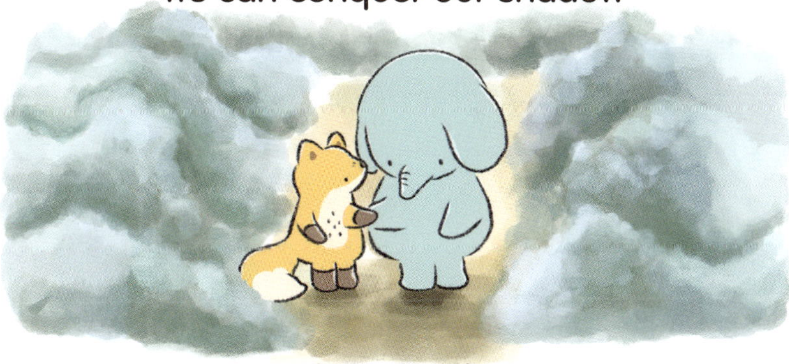

a step at a time

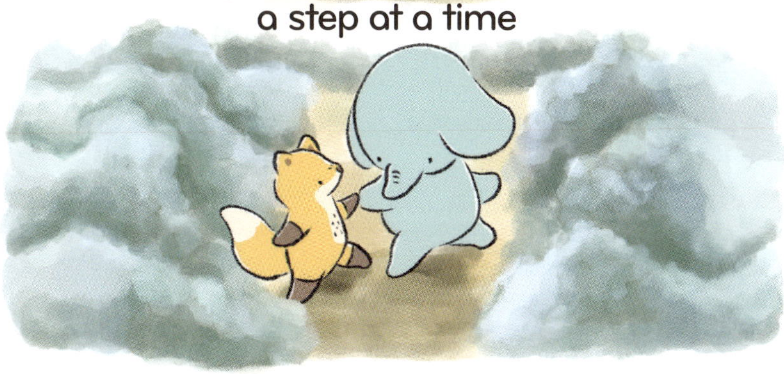

Let's make

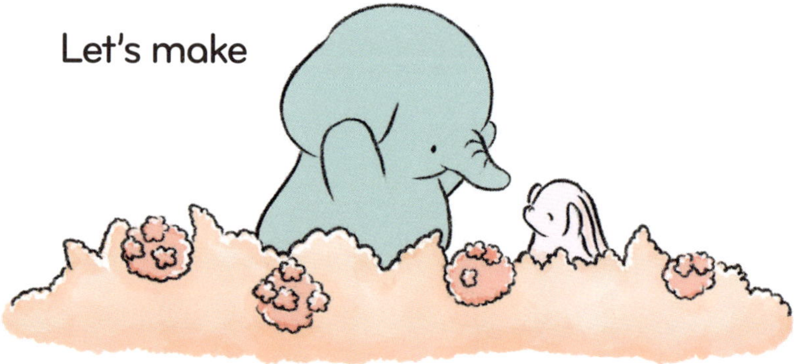

our stumble

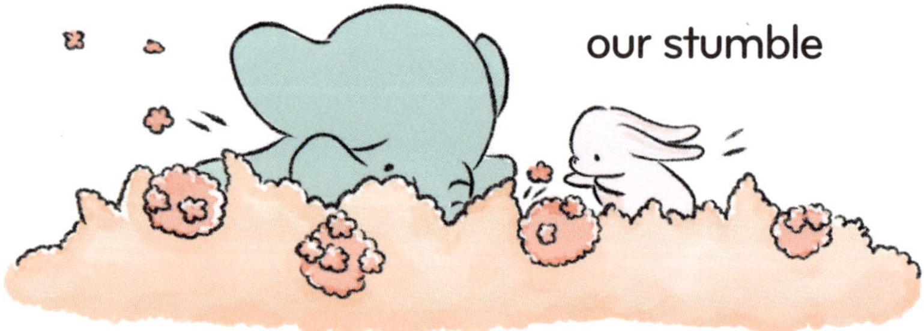

part of the dance!

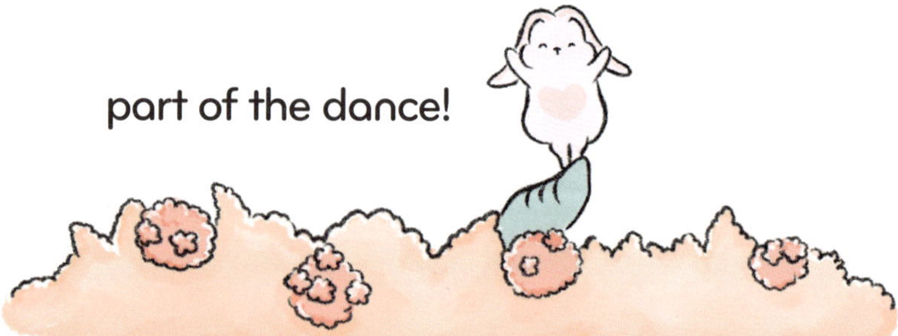

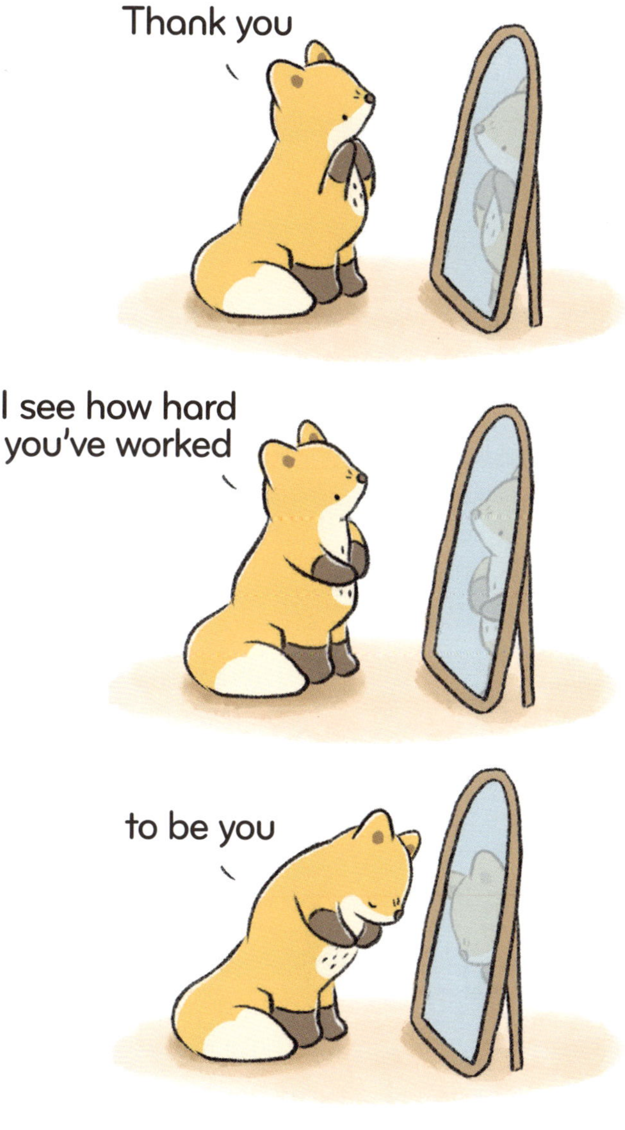
Thank you
I see how hard you've worked
to be you

Extra-ordinary Days

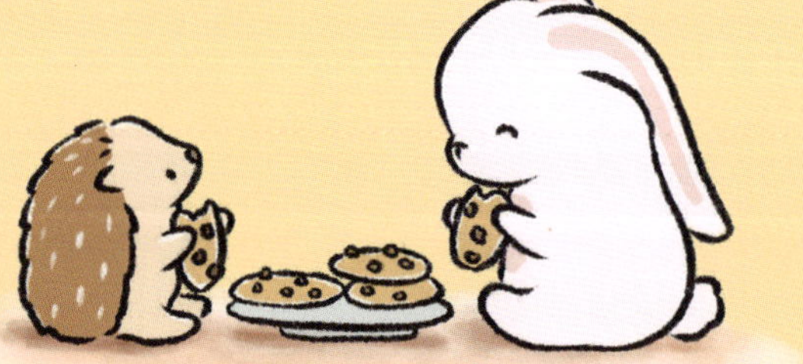

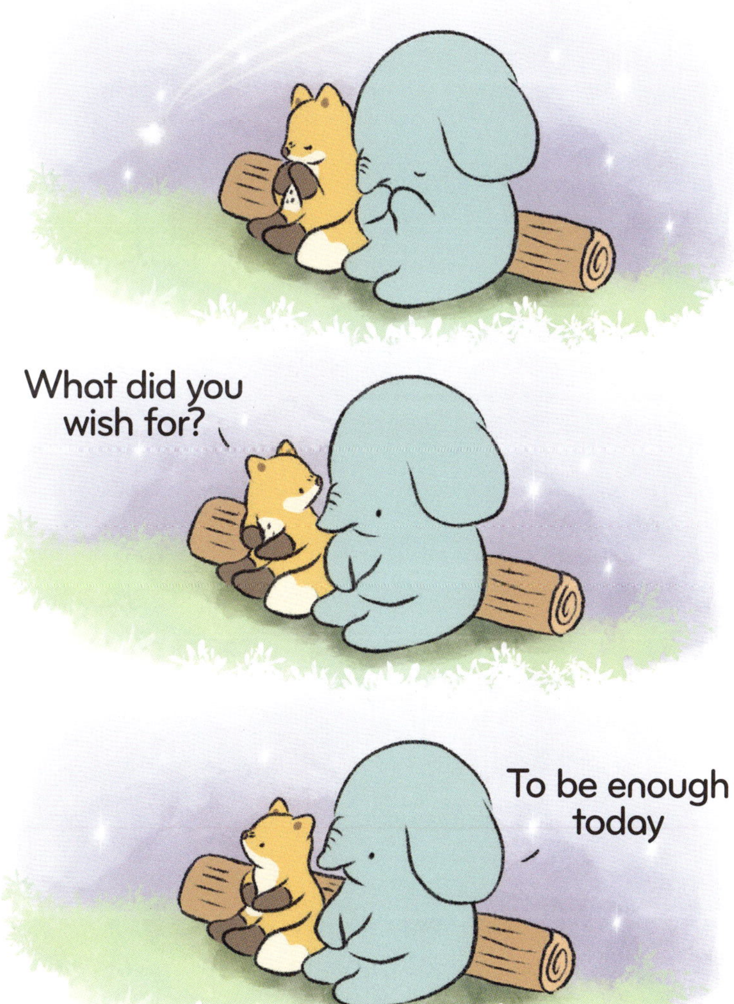
What did you wish for?
To be enough today

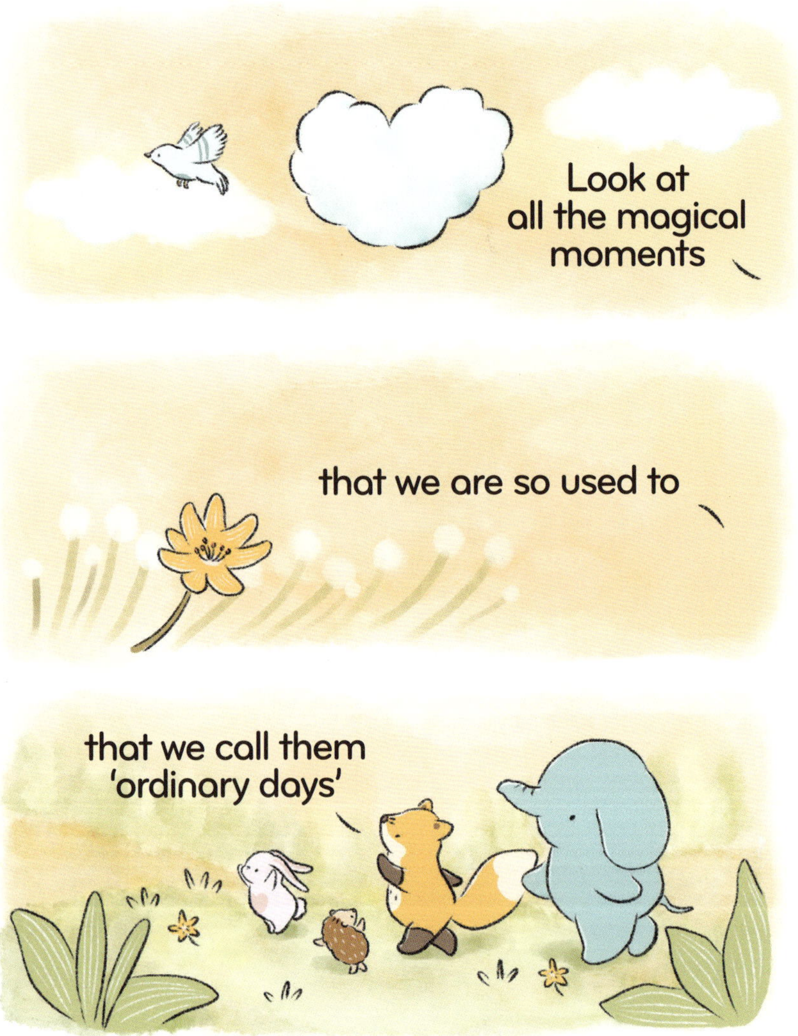
Look at
all the magical
moments
that we are so used to
that we call them
'ordinary days'

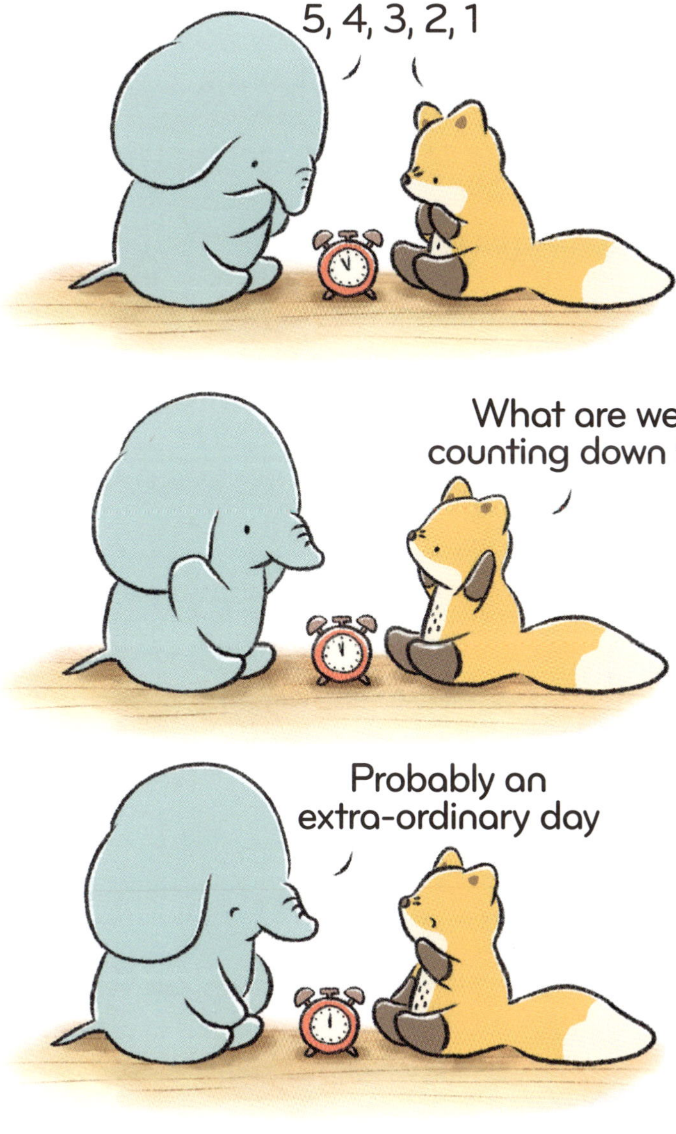

5, 4, 3, 2, 1
What are we counting down to?
Probably an extra-ordinary day

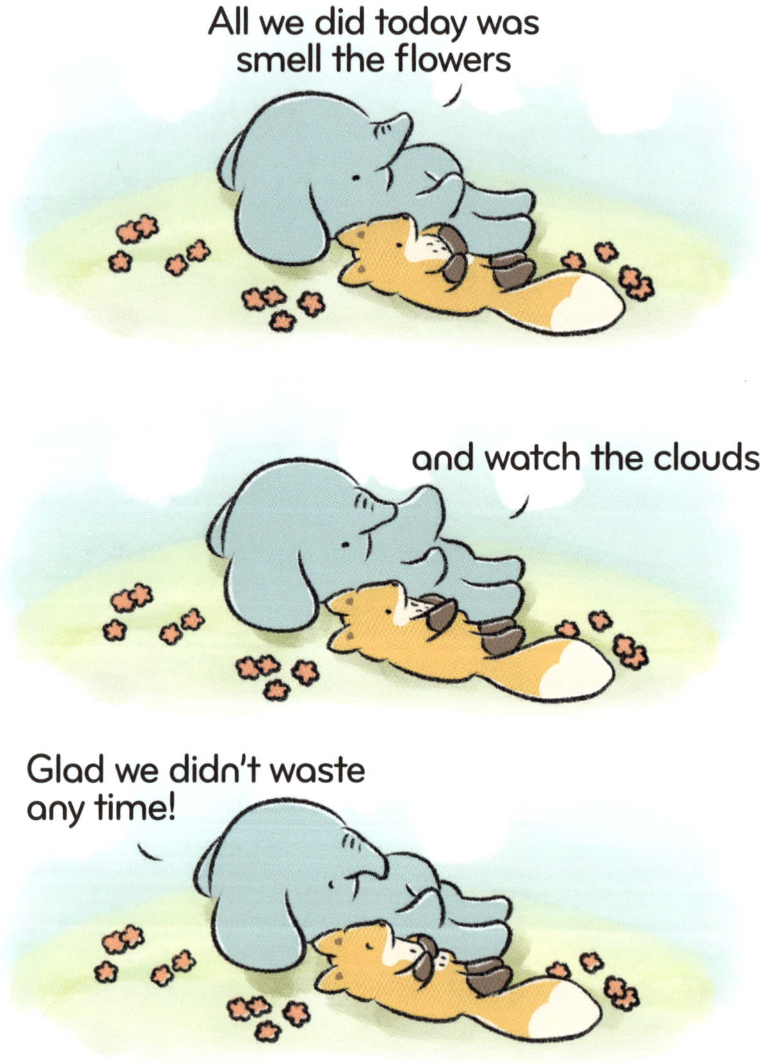
All we did today was smell the flowers
and watch the clouds
Glad we didn't waste any time!

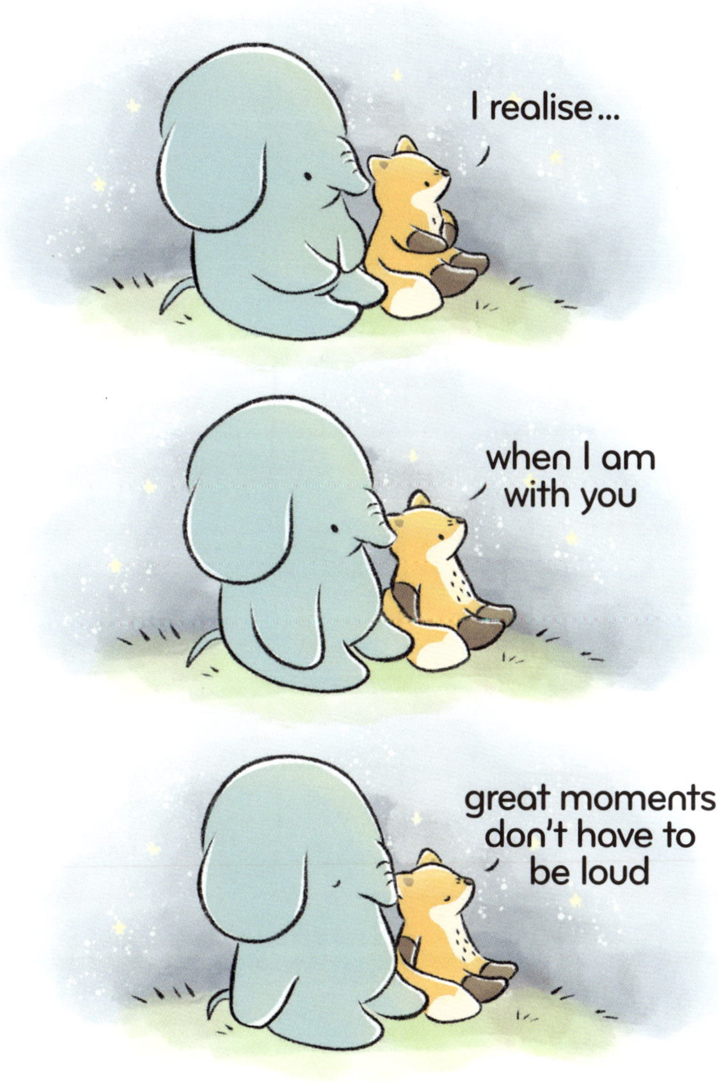
I realise...
when I am with you
great moments don't have to be loud

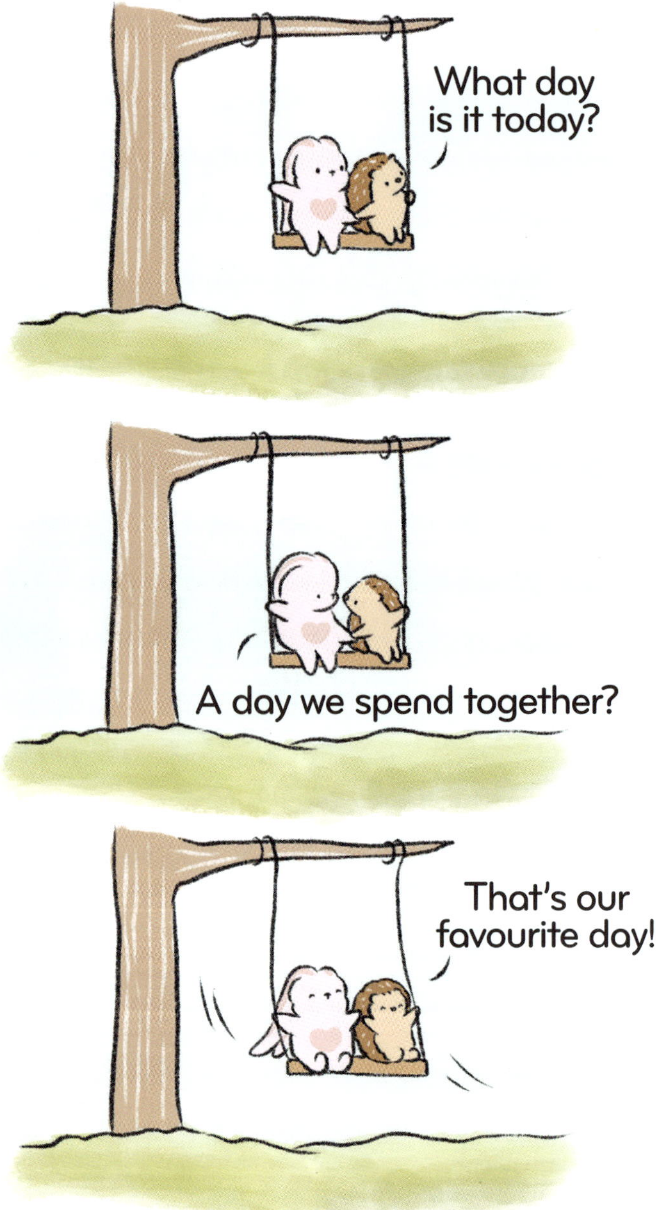
What day is it today?
A day we spend together?
That's our favourite day!

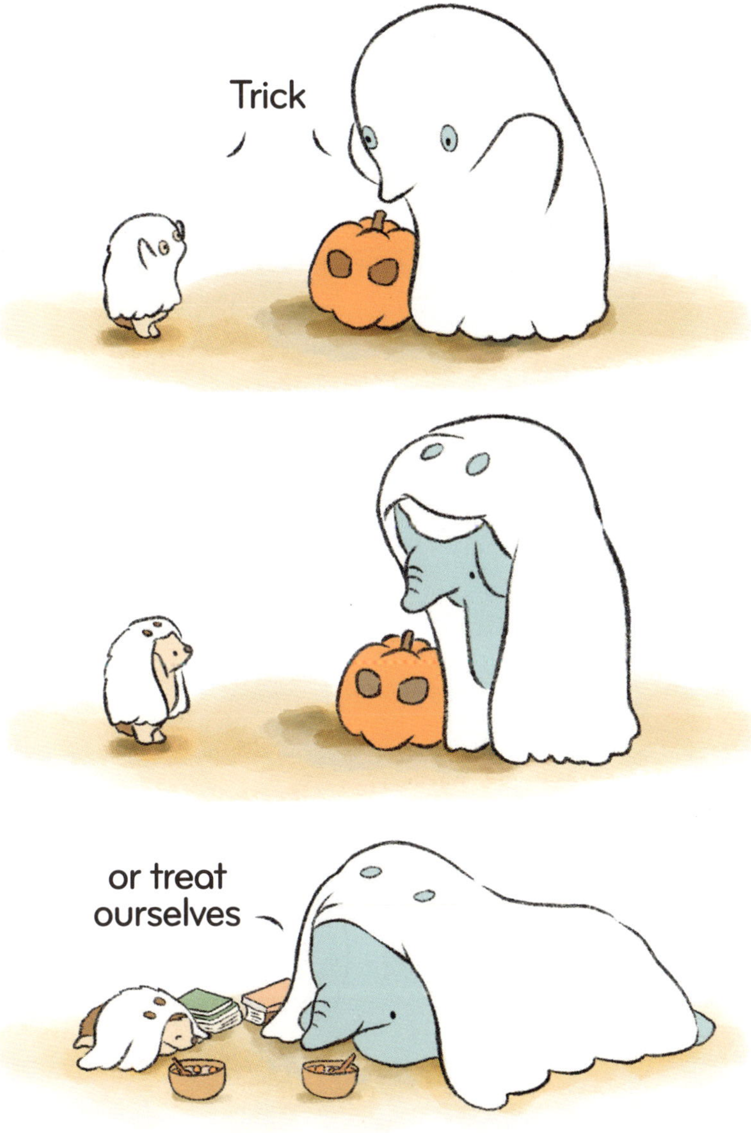
Trick
or treat
ourselves

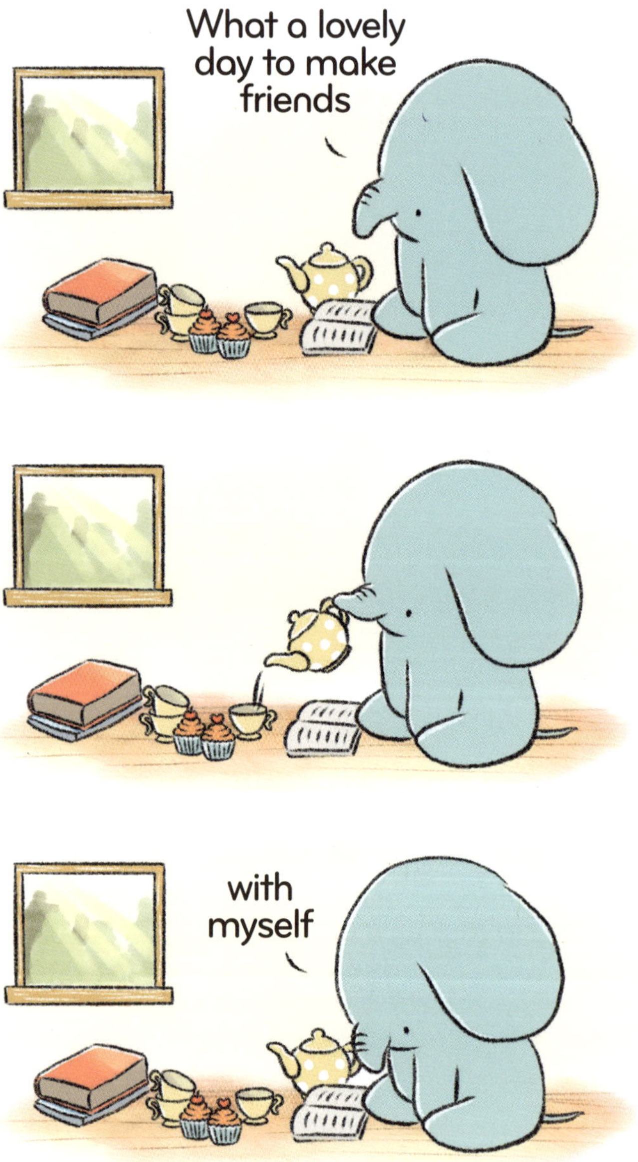
What a lovely day to make friends
with myself

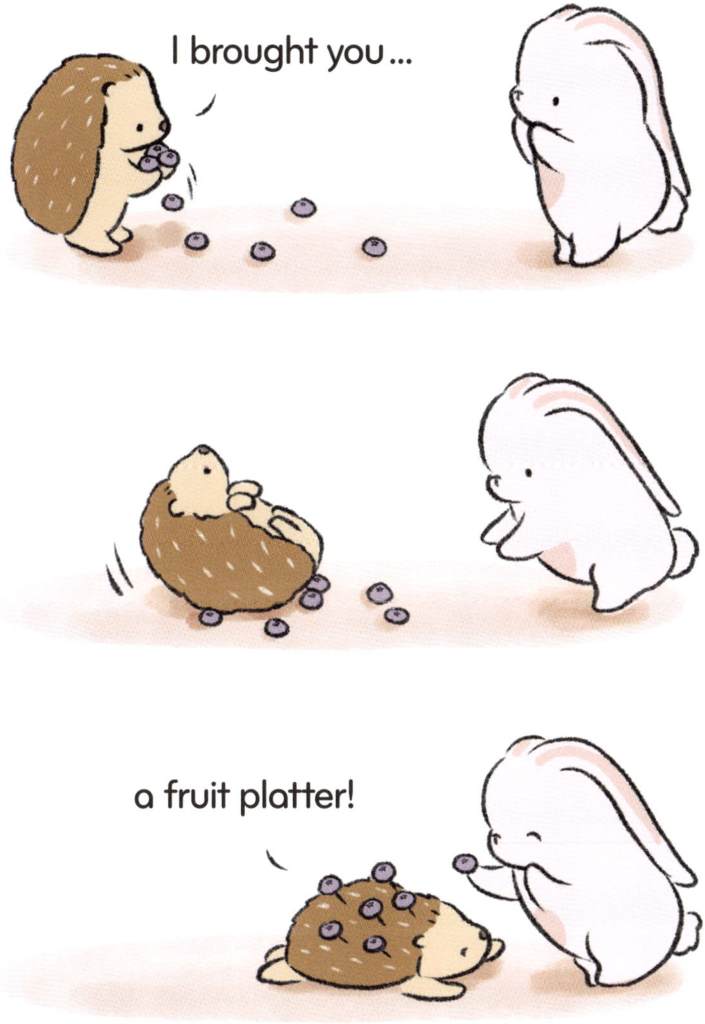
I brought you...
a fruit platter!

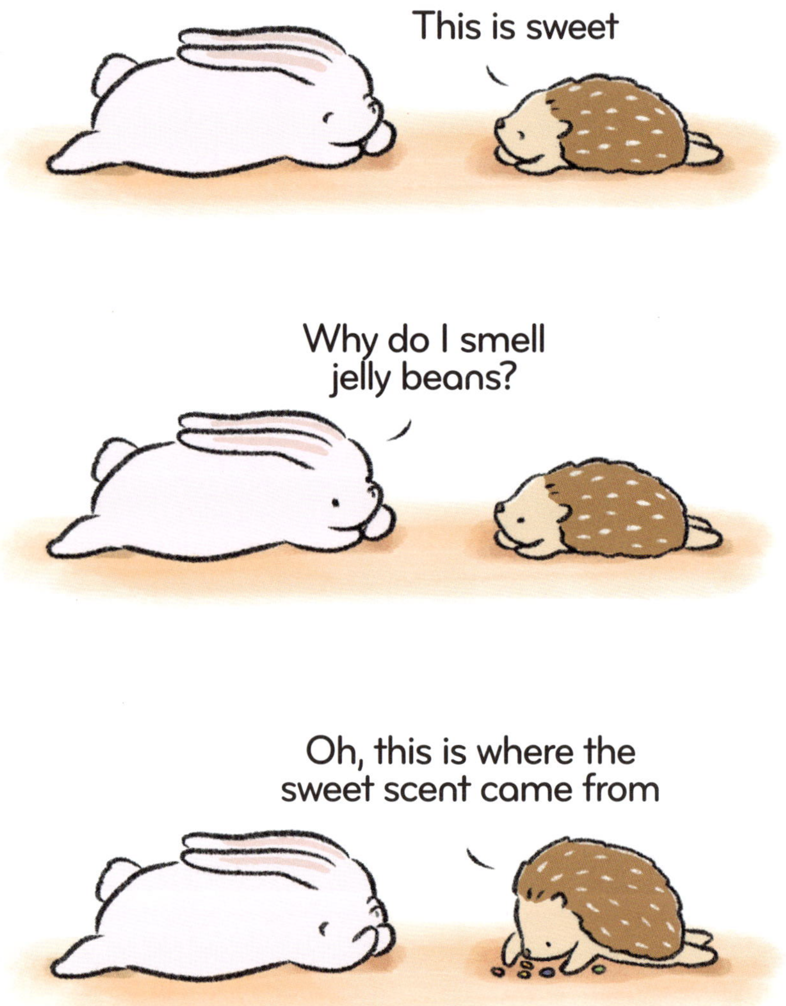
This is sweet
Why do I smell jelly beans?
Oh, this is where the sweet scent came from

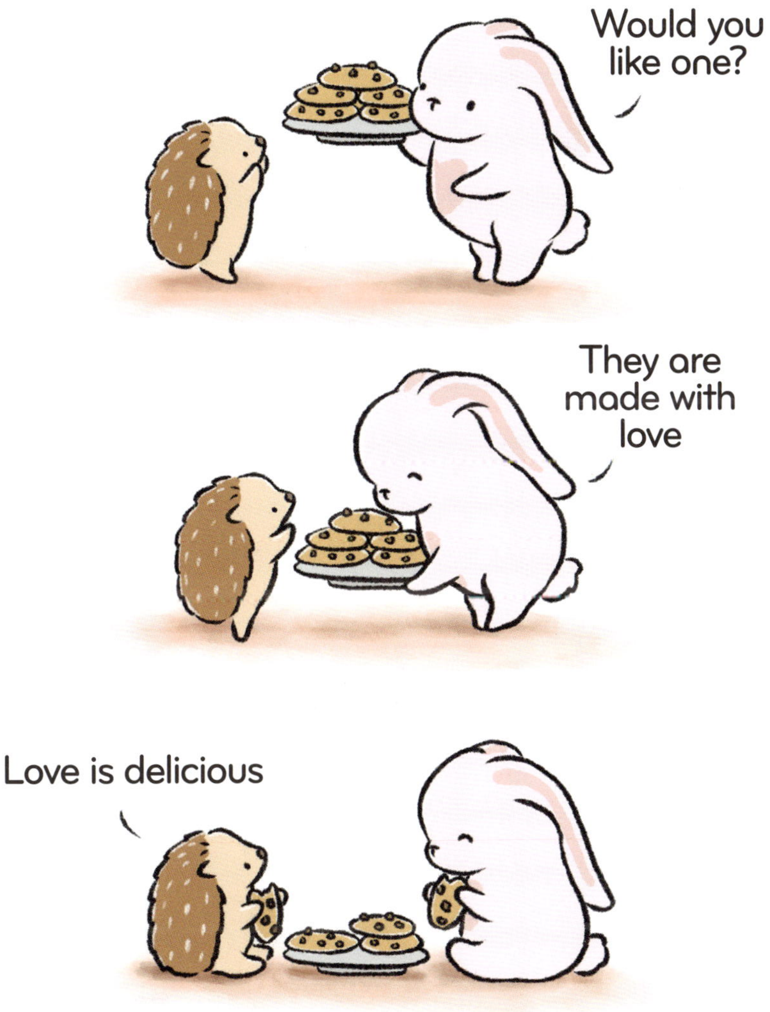
Would you like one?
They are made with love
Love is delicious

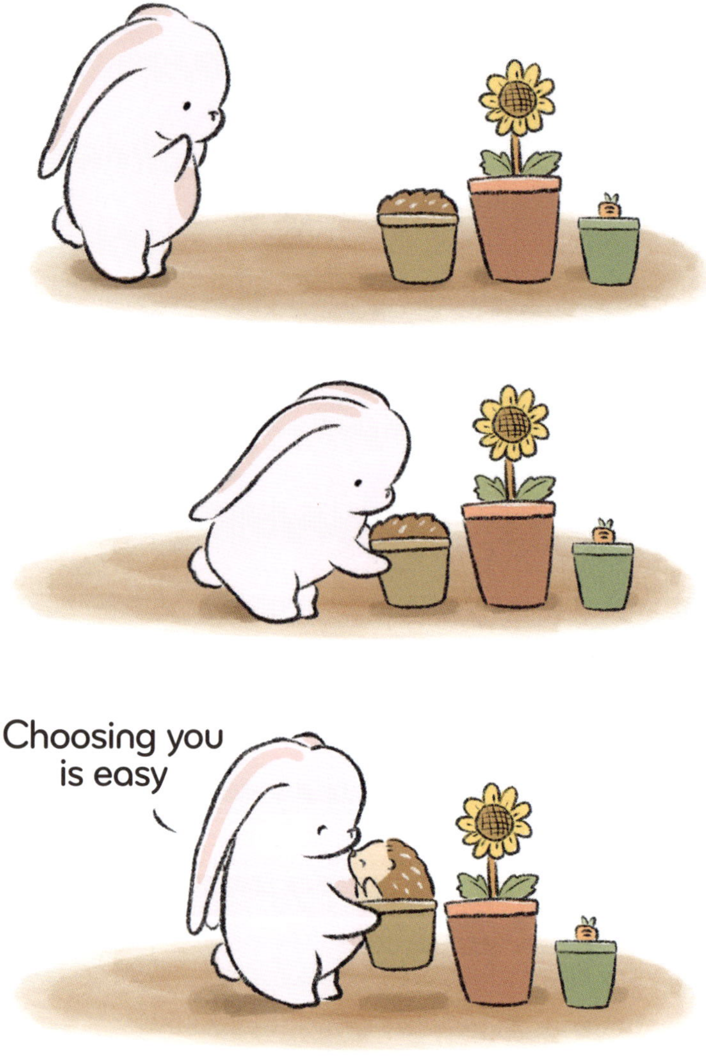
Choosing you
is easy

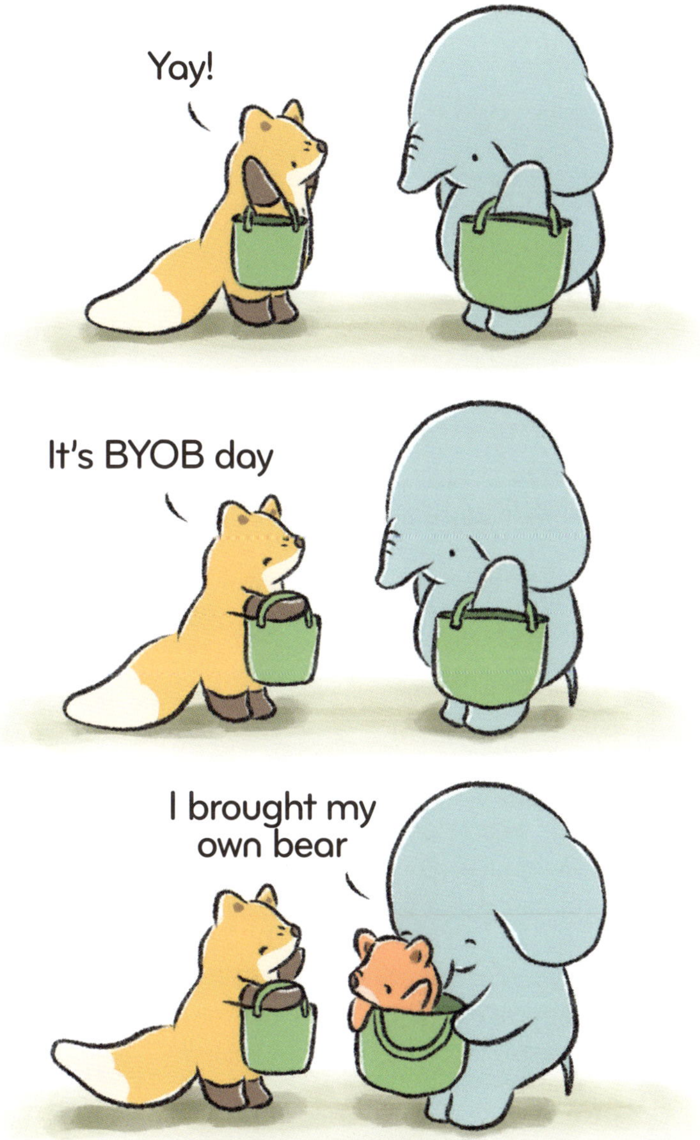
Yay!
It's BYOB day
I brought my own bear

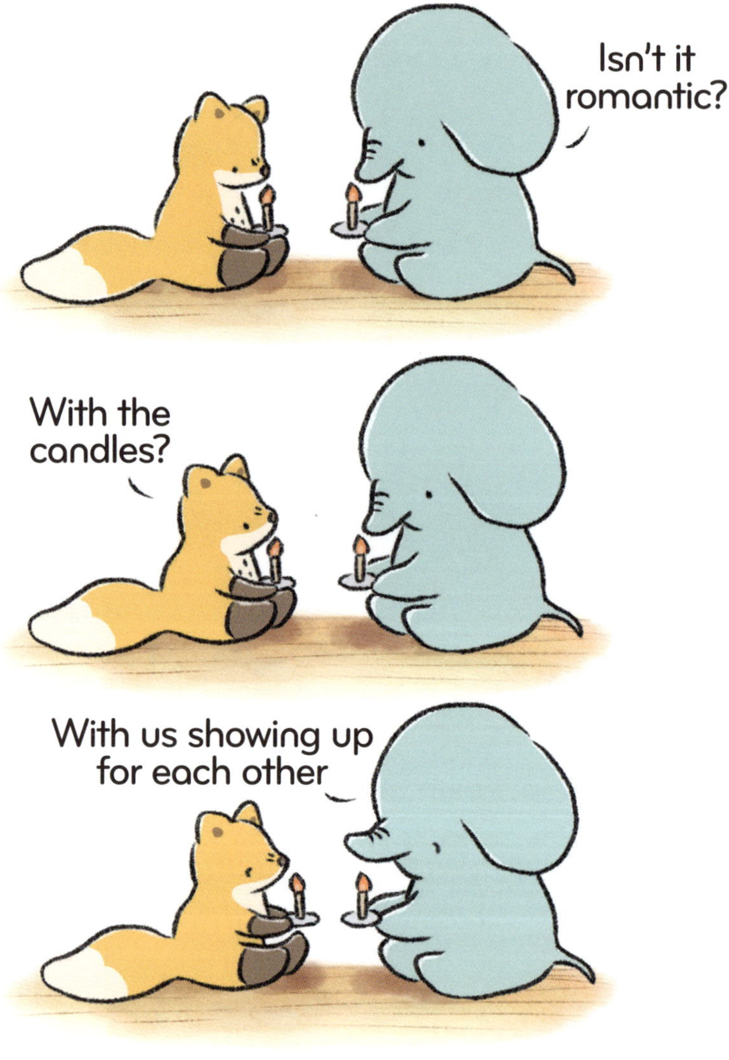
Isn't it
romantic?
With the
candles?
With us showing up
for each other

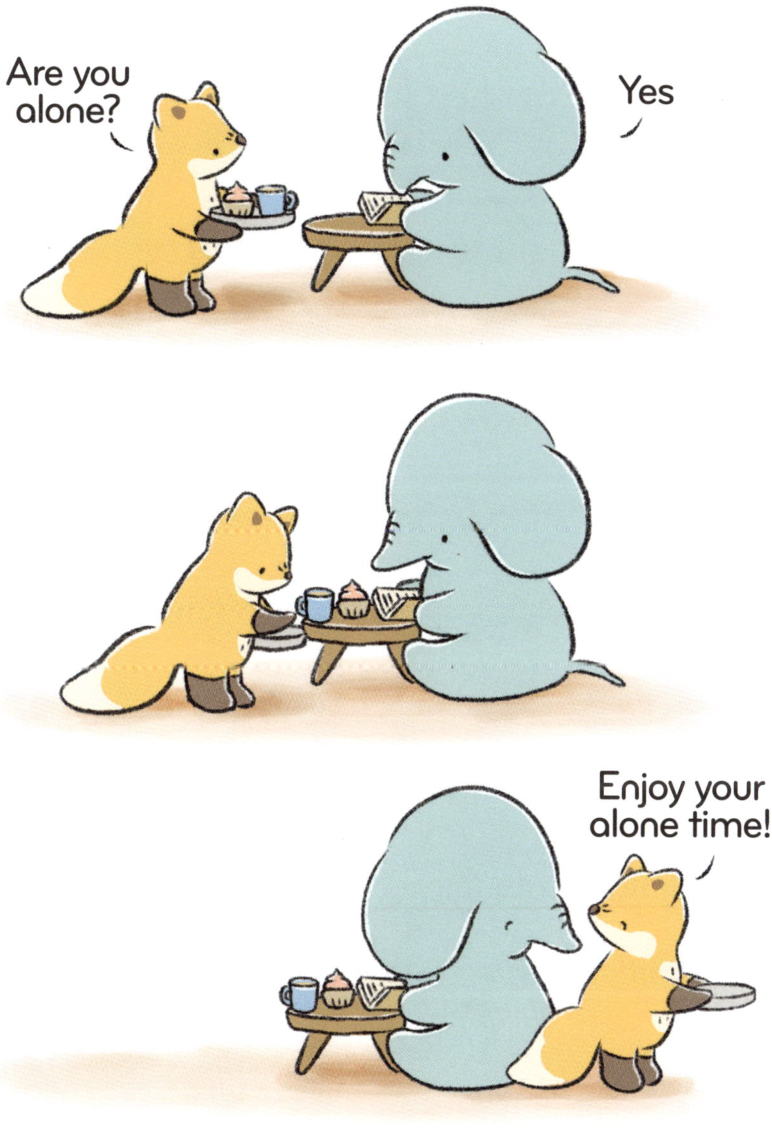
Are you alone?
Yes
Enjoy your alone time!

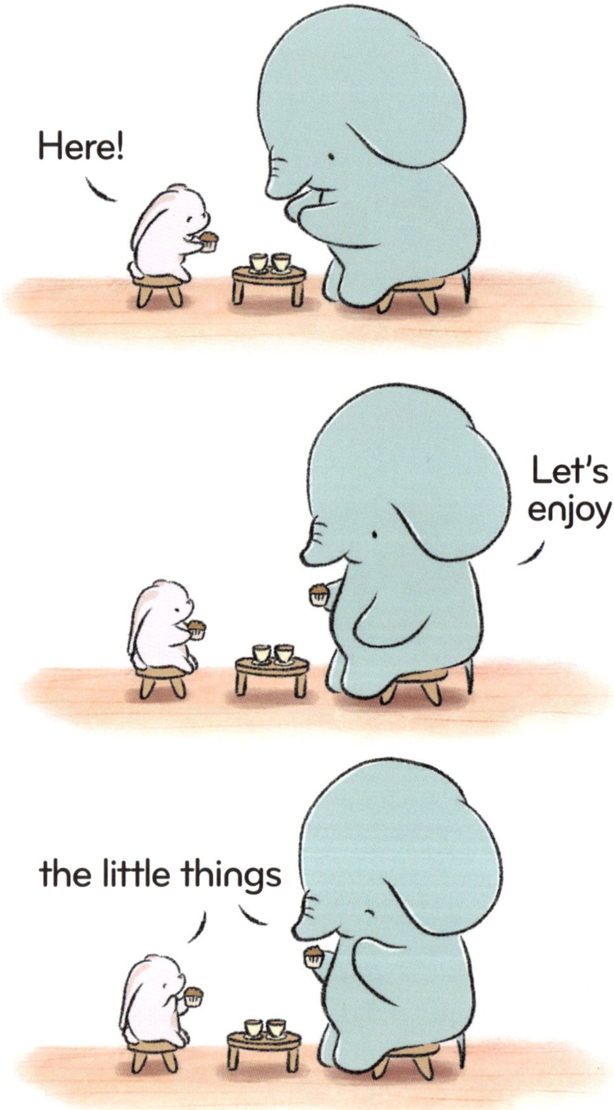
Here!
Let's enjoy
the little things

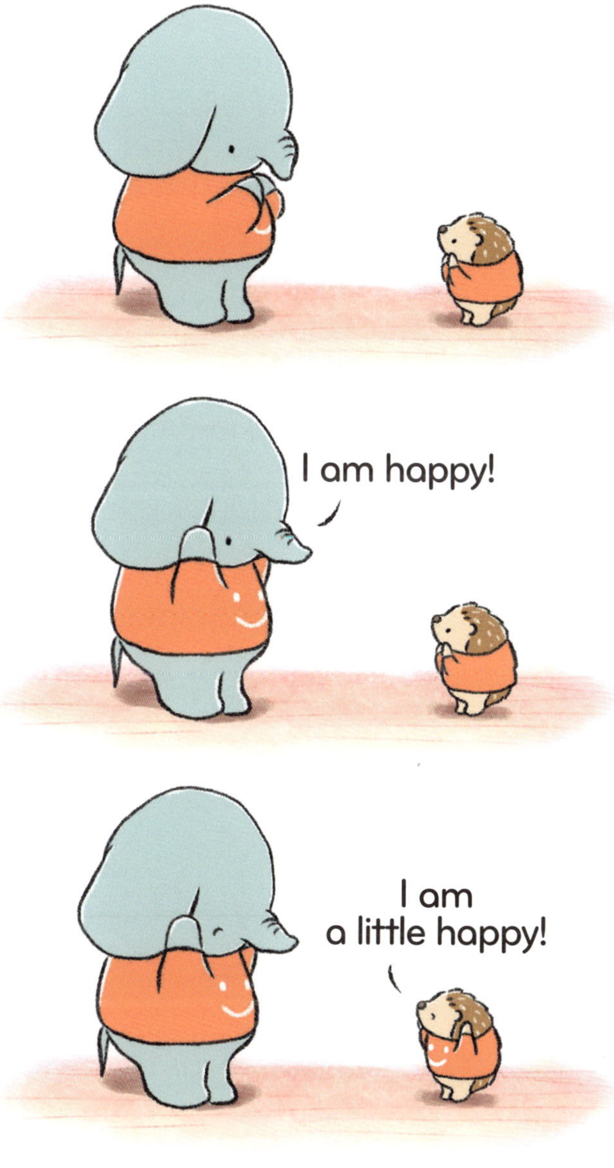
I am happy!
I am
a little happy!

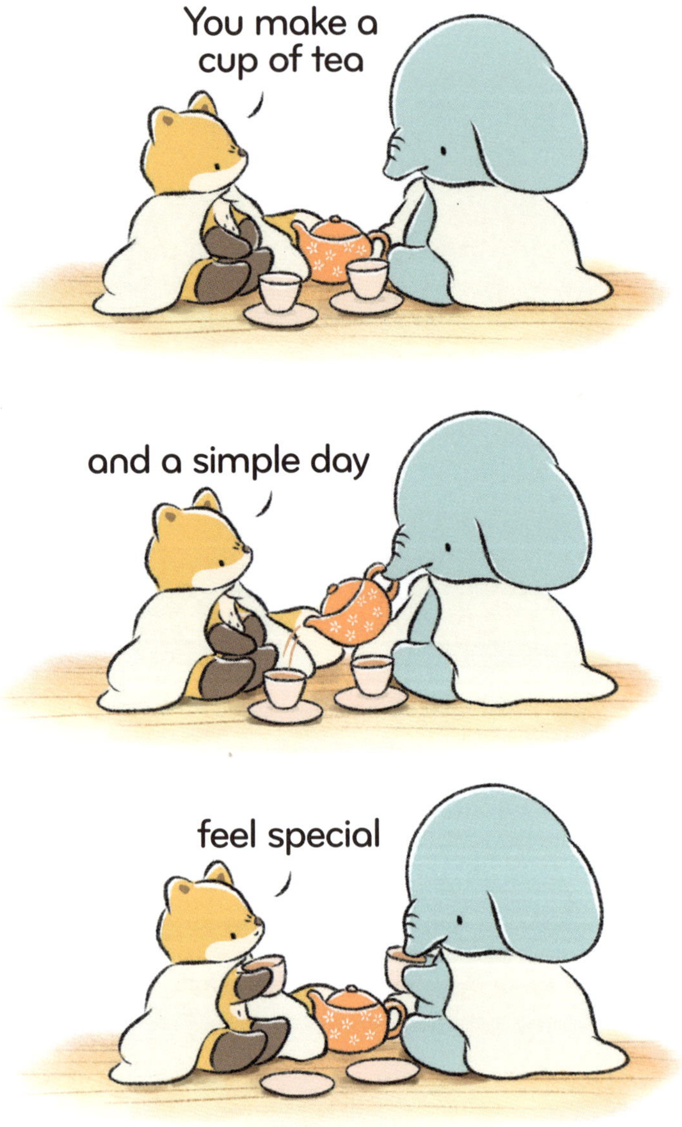
You make a
cup of tea
and a simple day
feel special

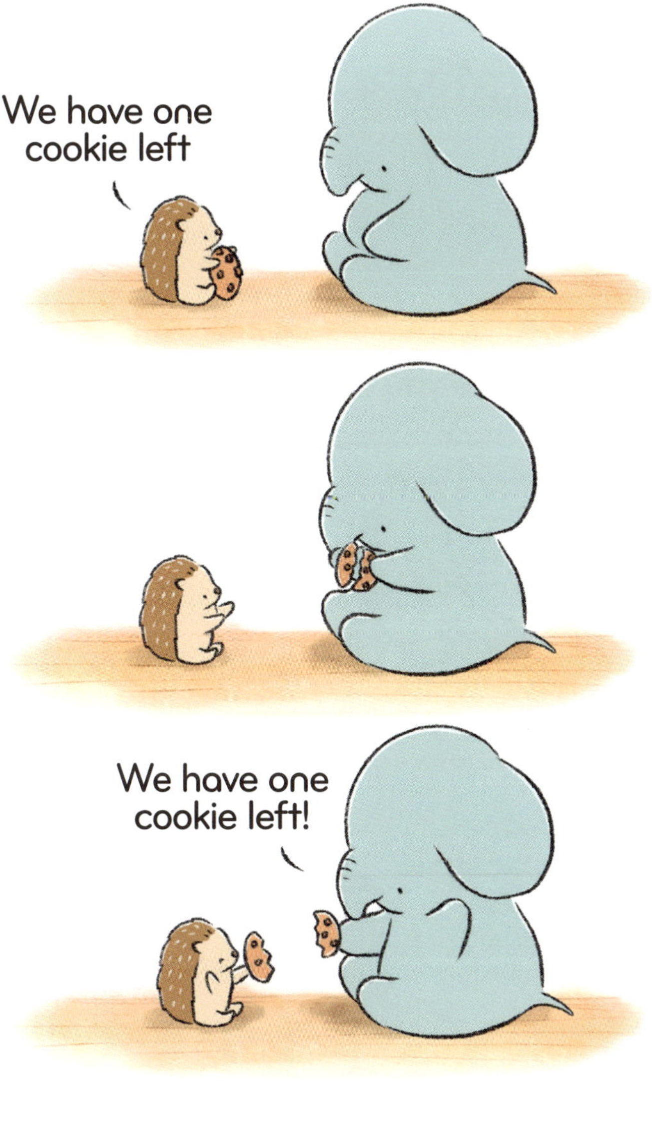
We have one cookie left
We have one cookie left!

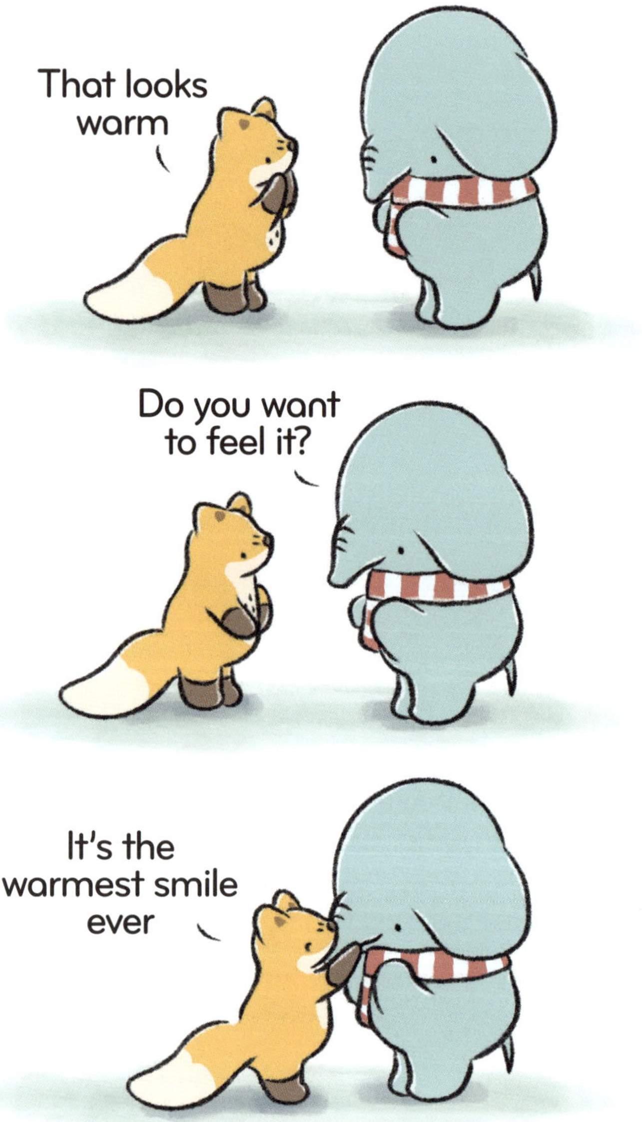
That looks warm
Do you want to feel it?
It's the warmest smile ever

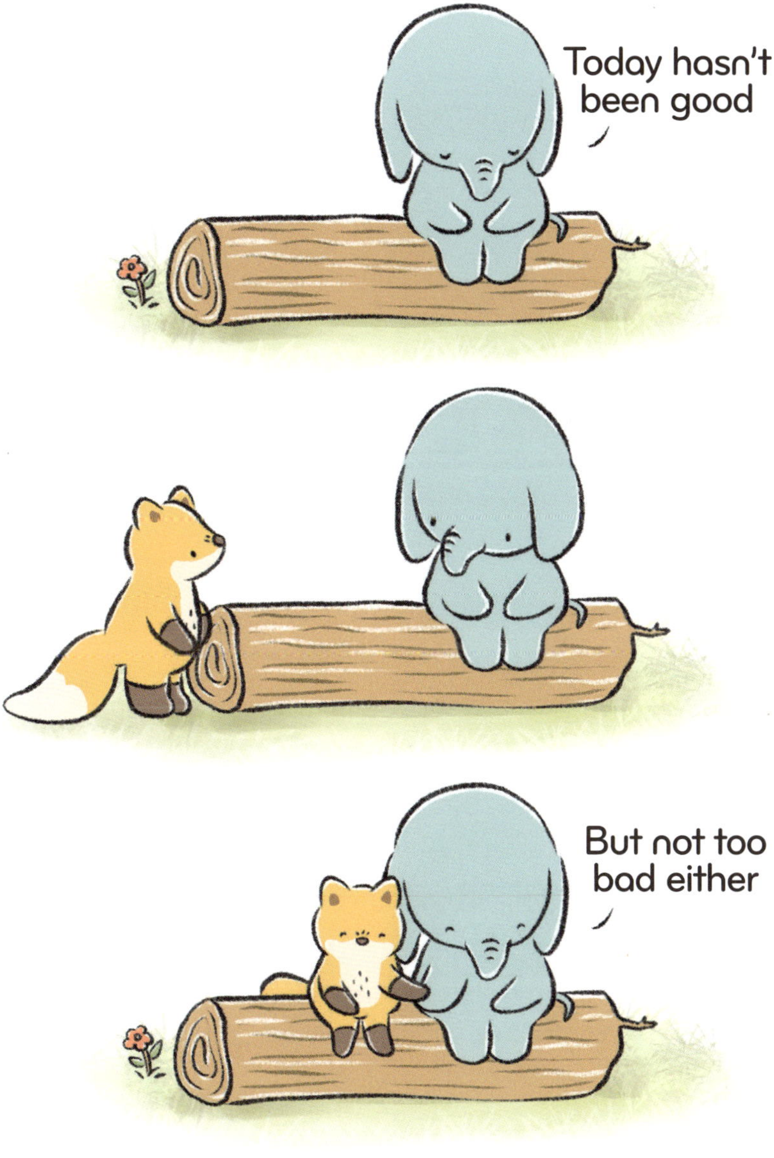
Today hasn't
been good
But not too
bad either

Thank You for Existing

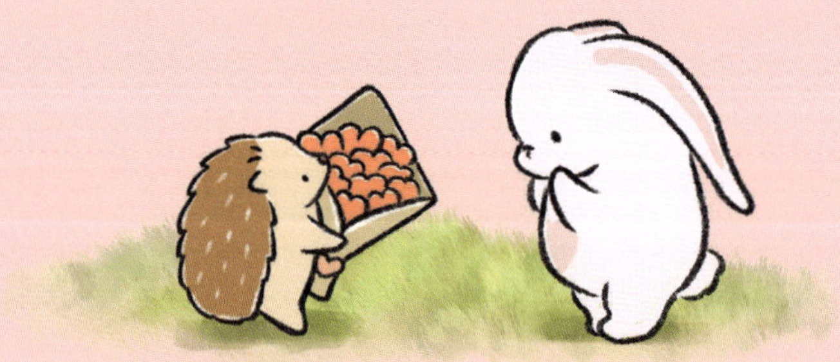

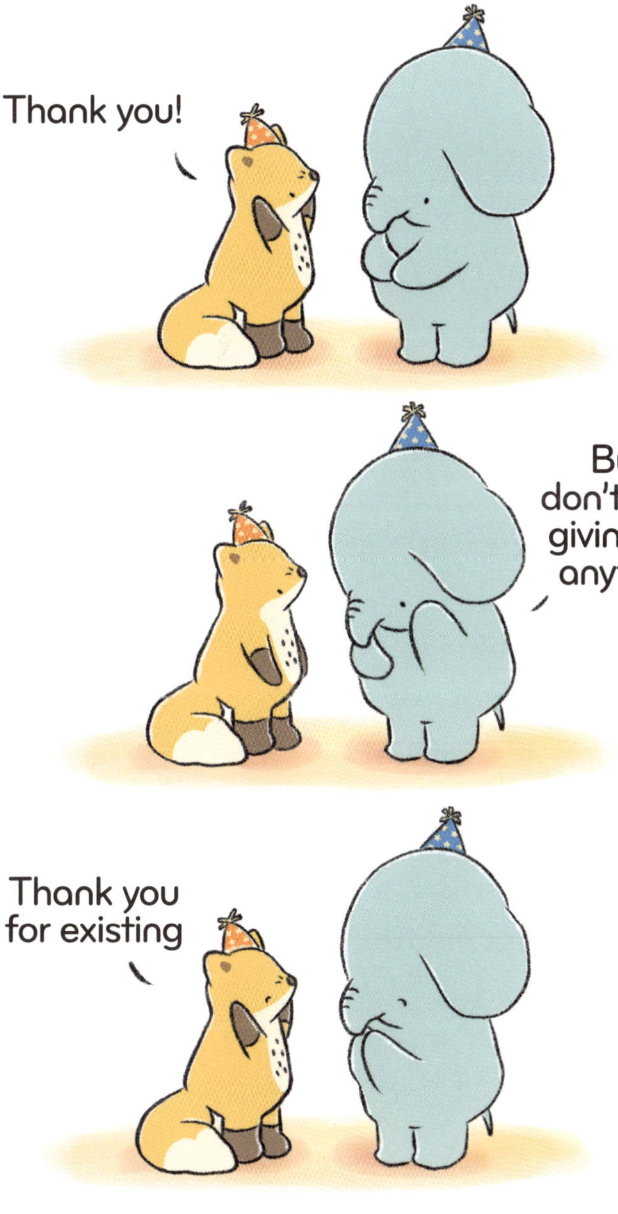
Thank you!
But I don't recall giving you anything
Thank you for existing

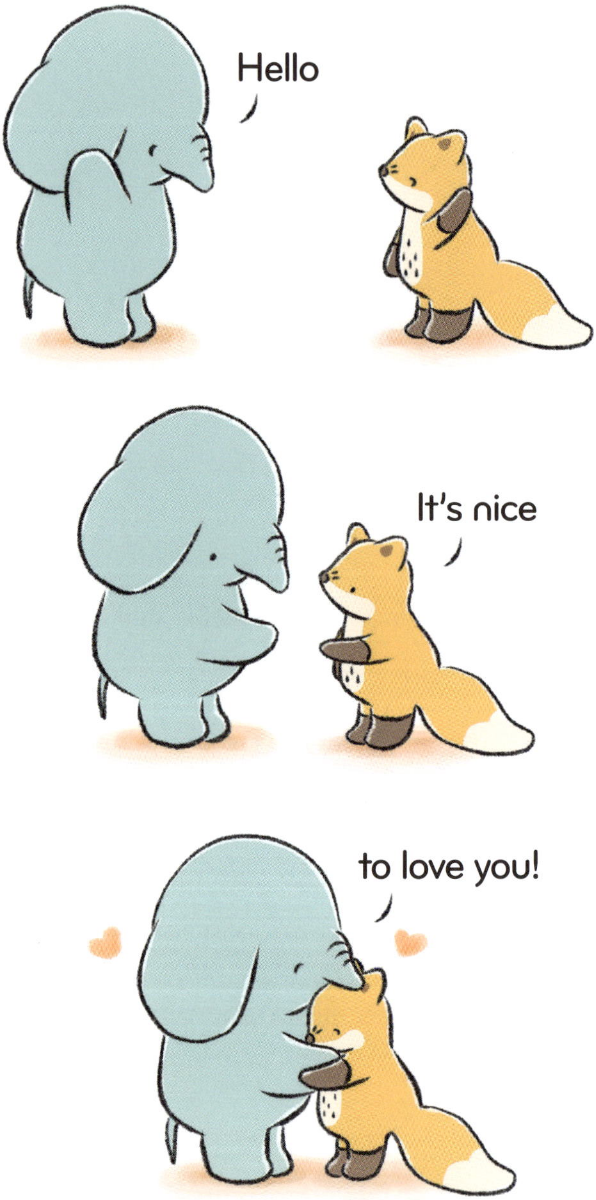
Hello
It's nice
to love you!

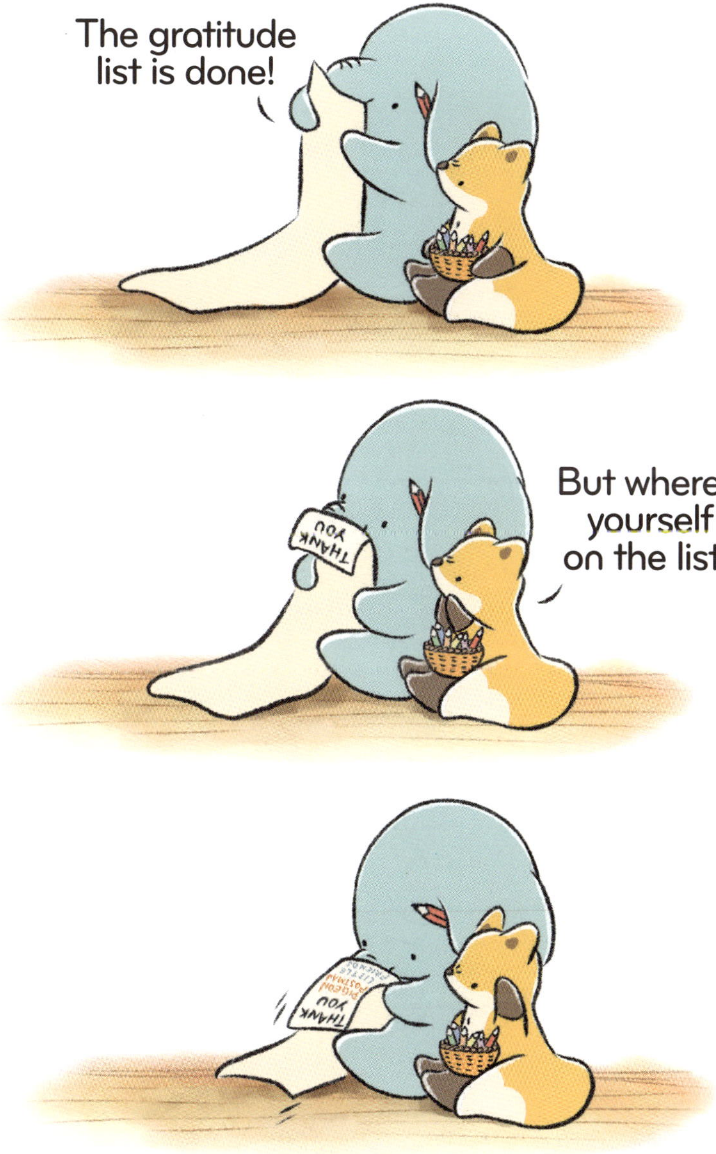
The gratitude list is done!
But where's yourself on the list?

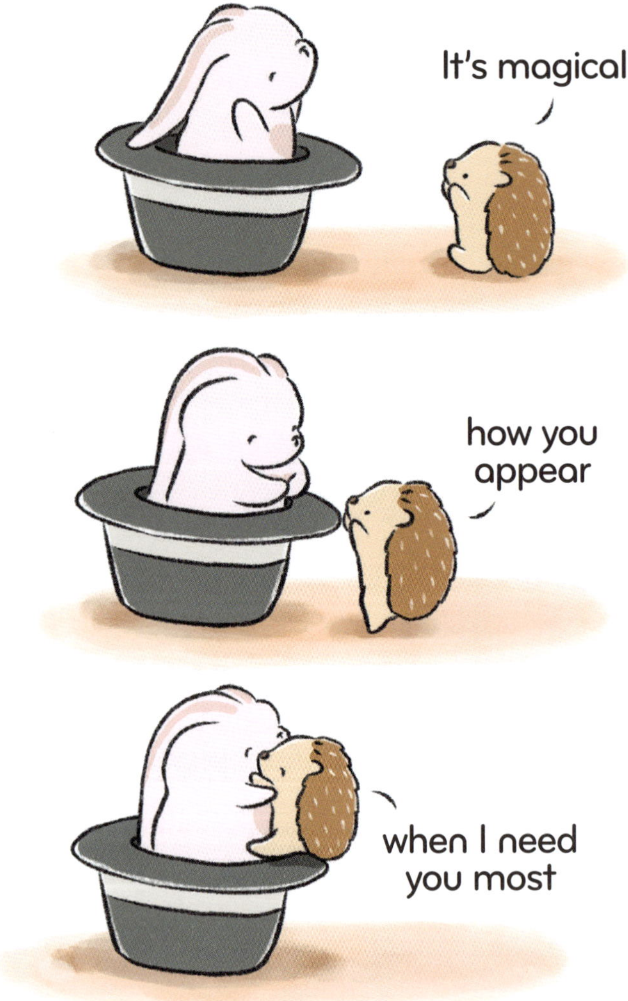
It's magical
how you appear
when I need you most

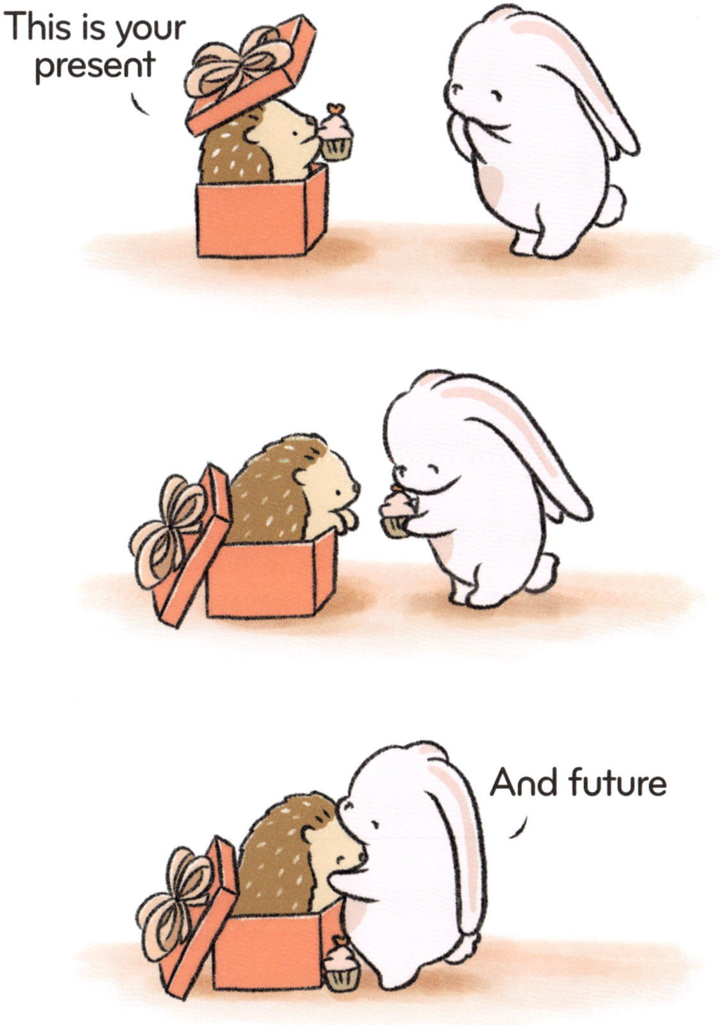
This is your present
And future

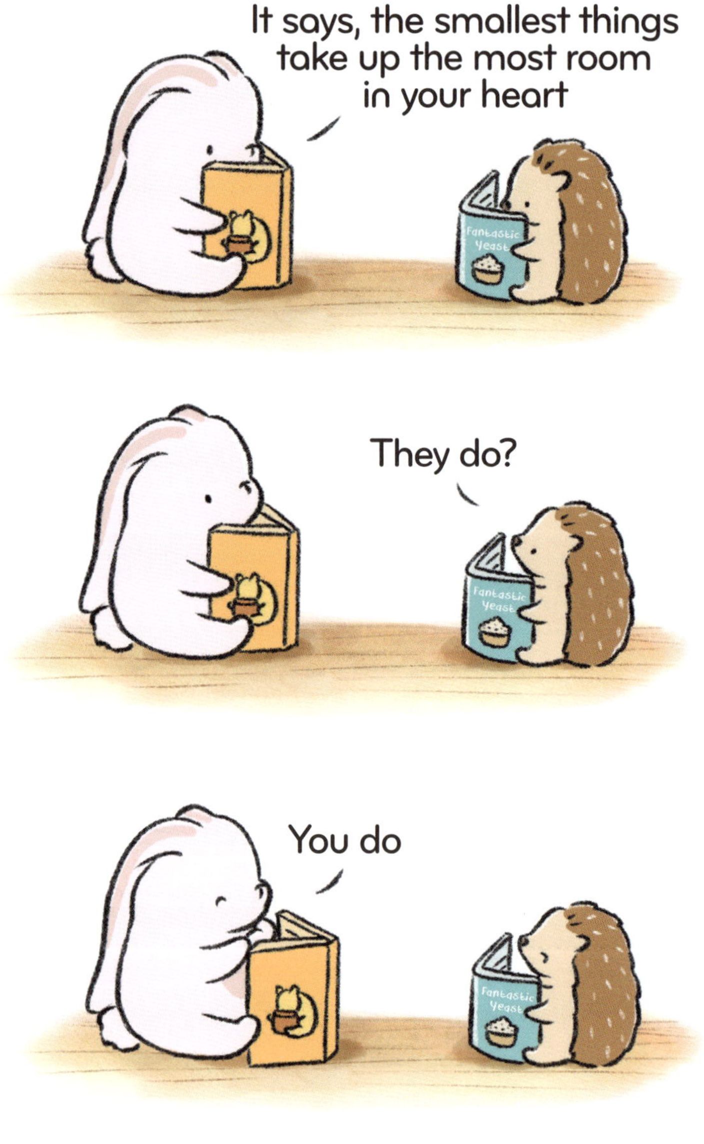
It says, the smallest things take up the most room in your heart
Fantastic Yeast
They do?
You do

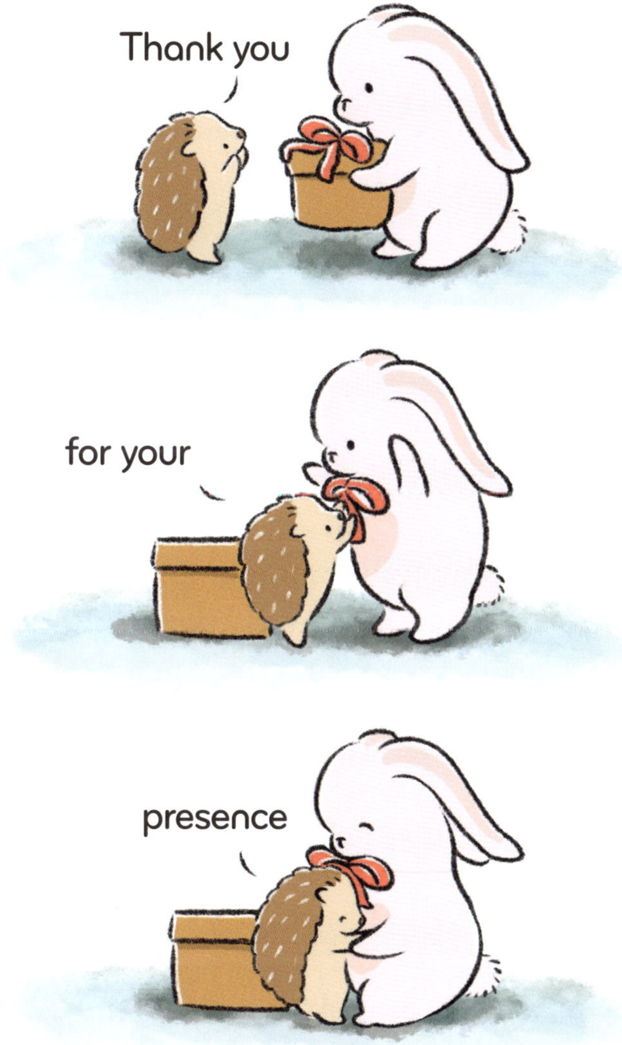
Thank you
for your
presence

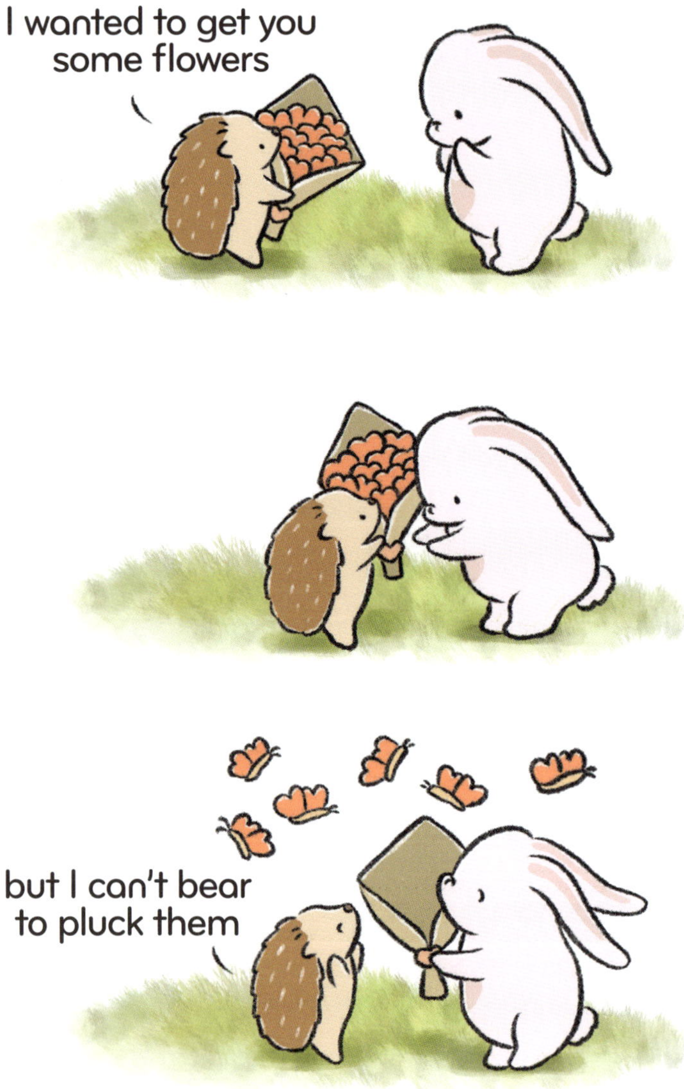
I wanted to get you some flowers
but I can't bear to pluck them

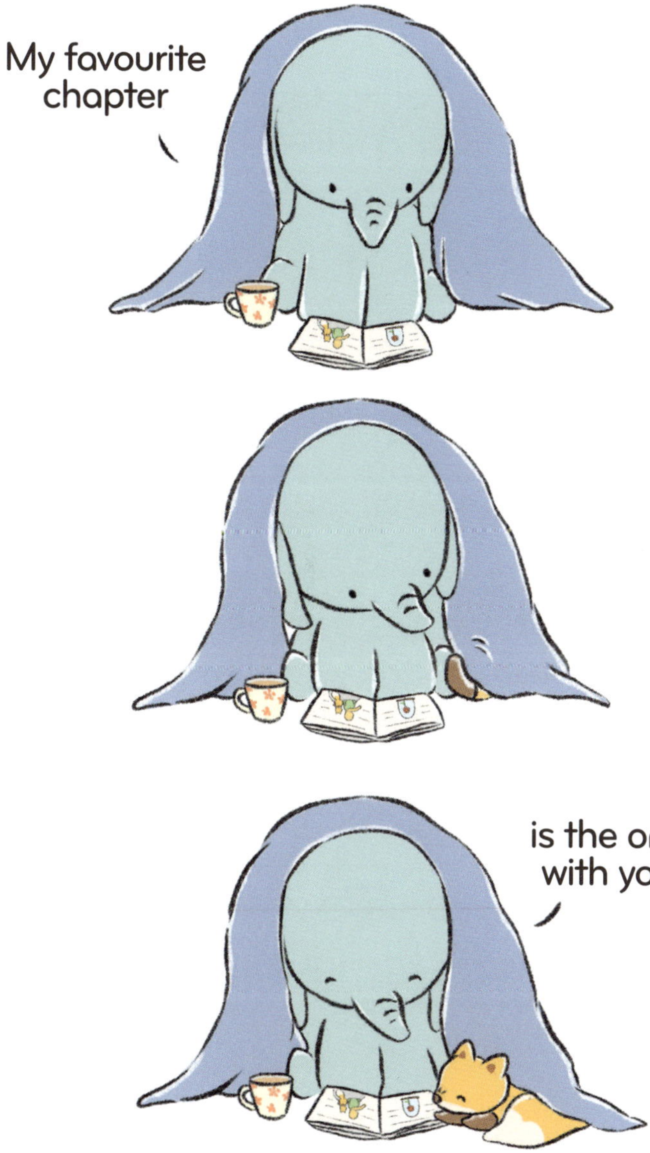
My favourite chapter
is the one with you

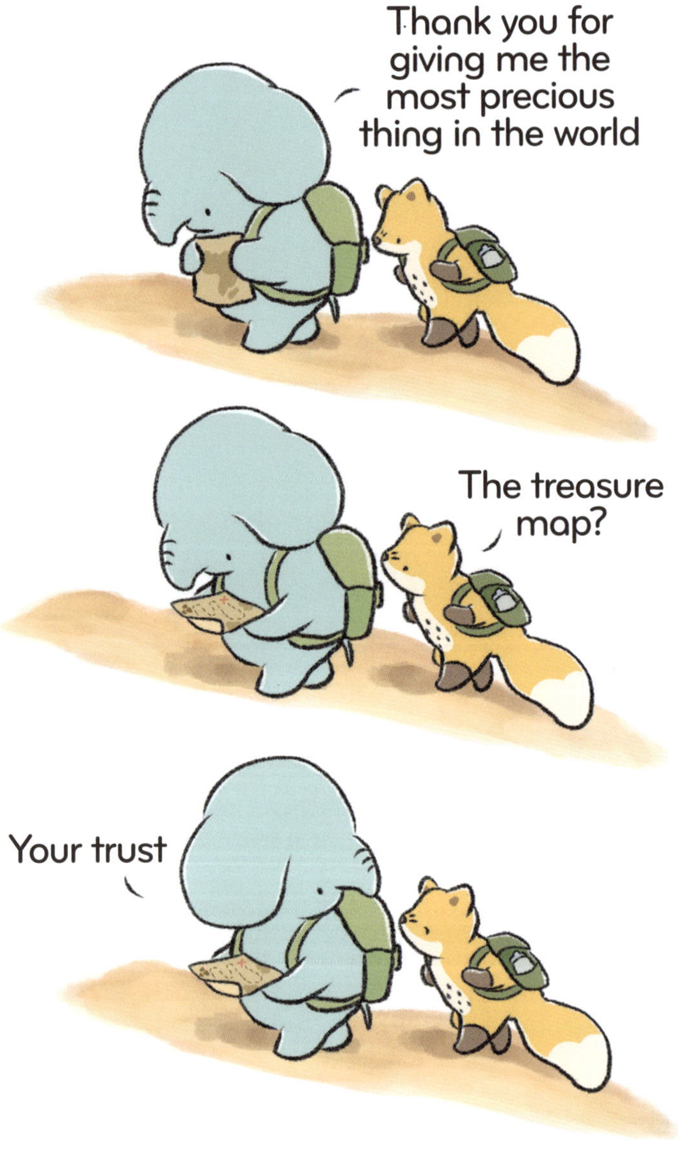
Thank you for giving me the most precious thing in the world
The treasure map?
Your trust

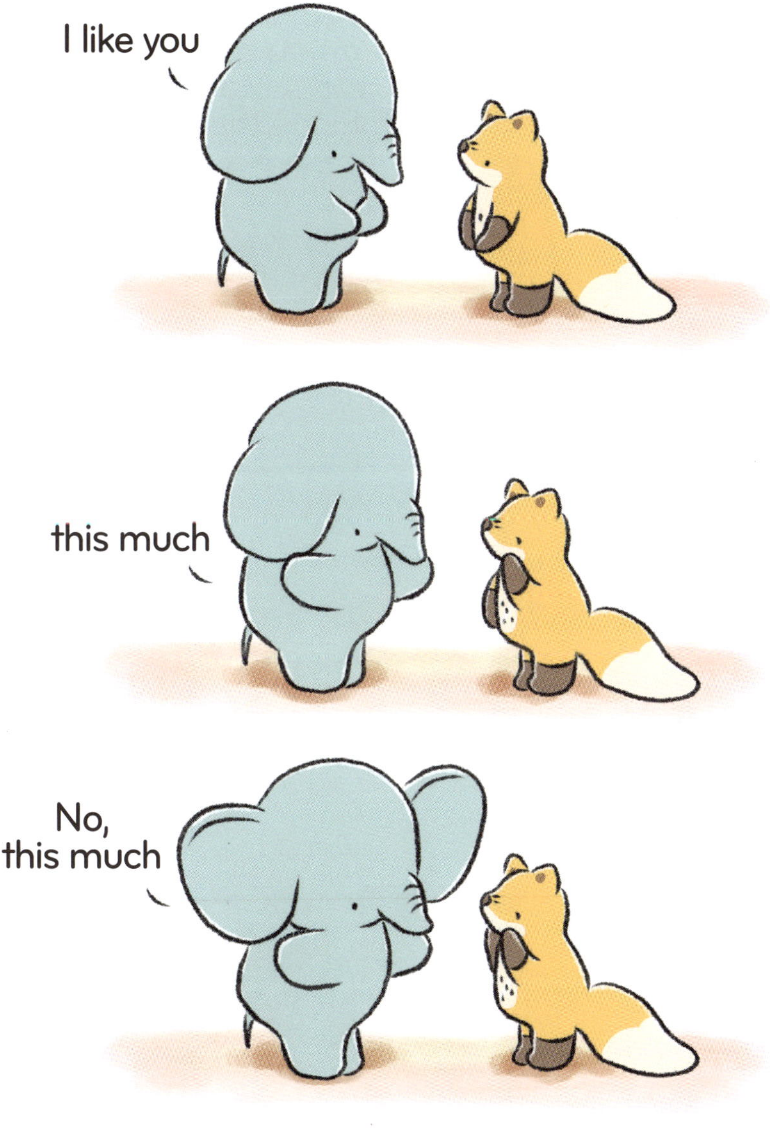
I like you
this much
No,
this much

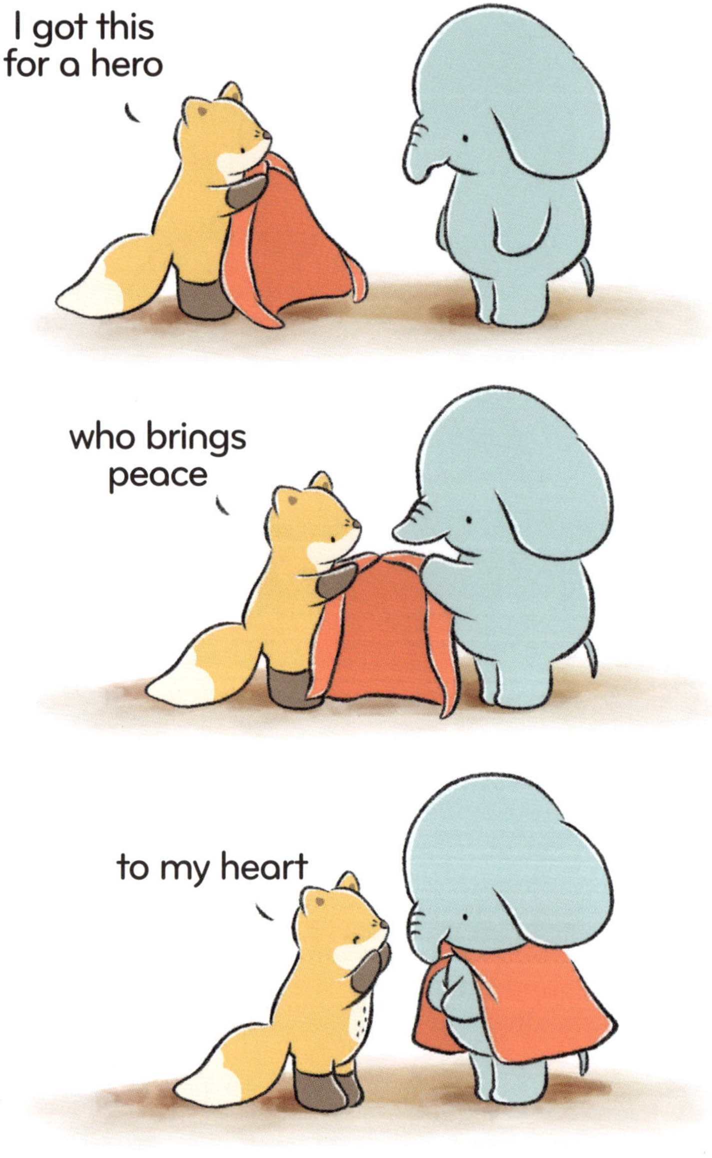
I got this
for a hero
who brings
peace
to my heart

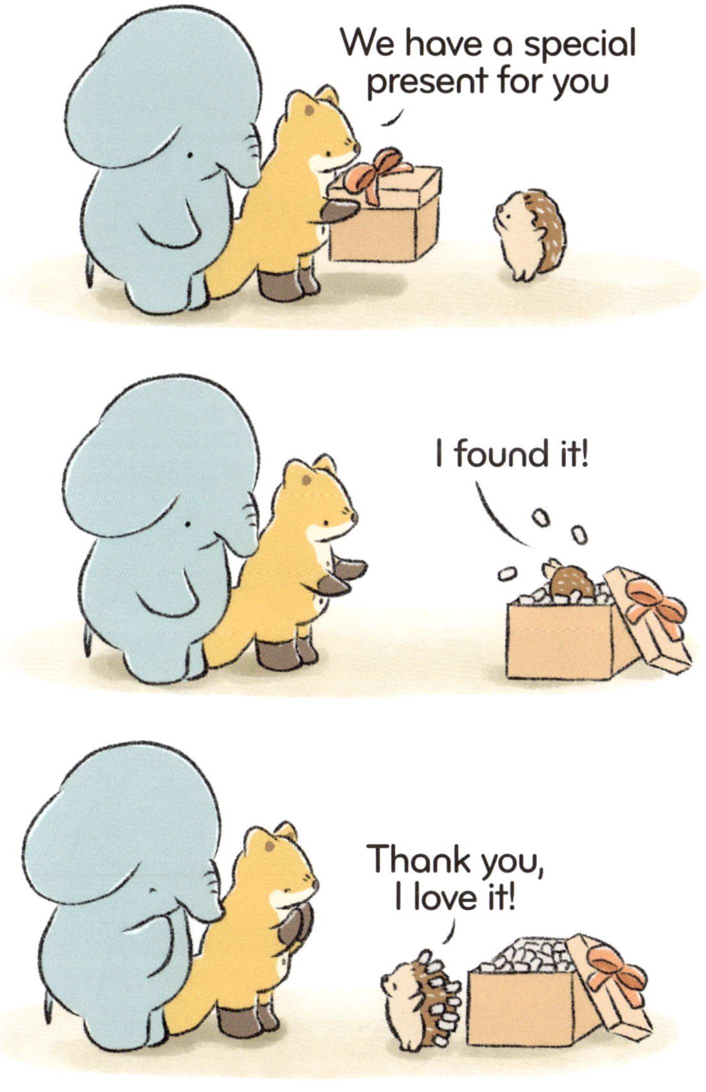
We have a special present for you
I found it!
Thank you, I love it!

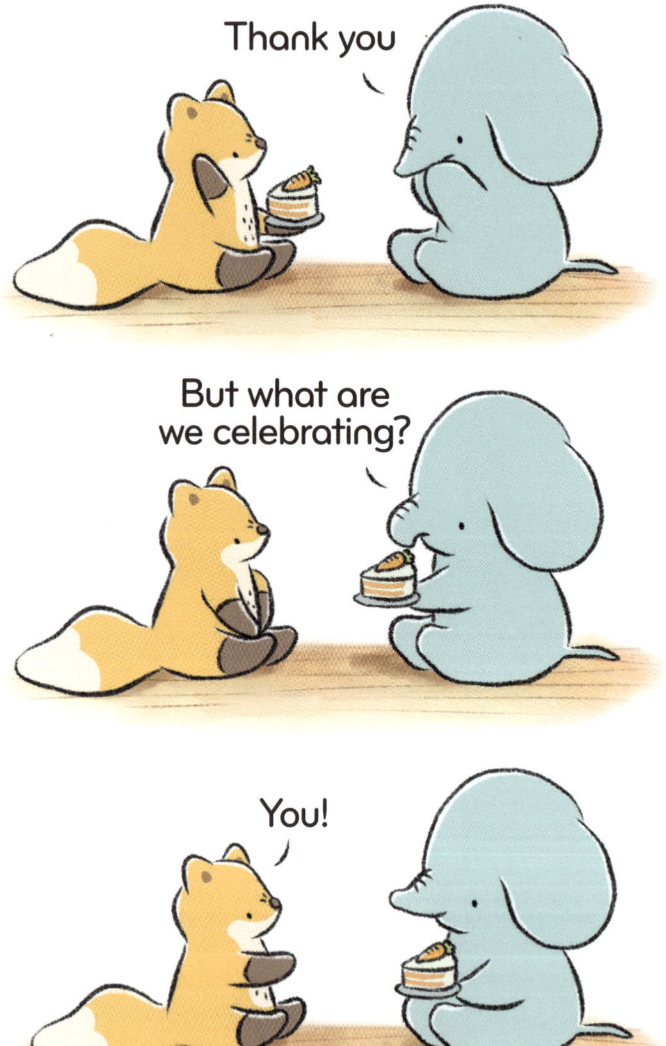
Thank you
But what are
we celebrating?
You!

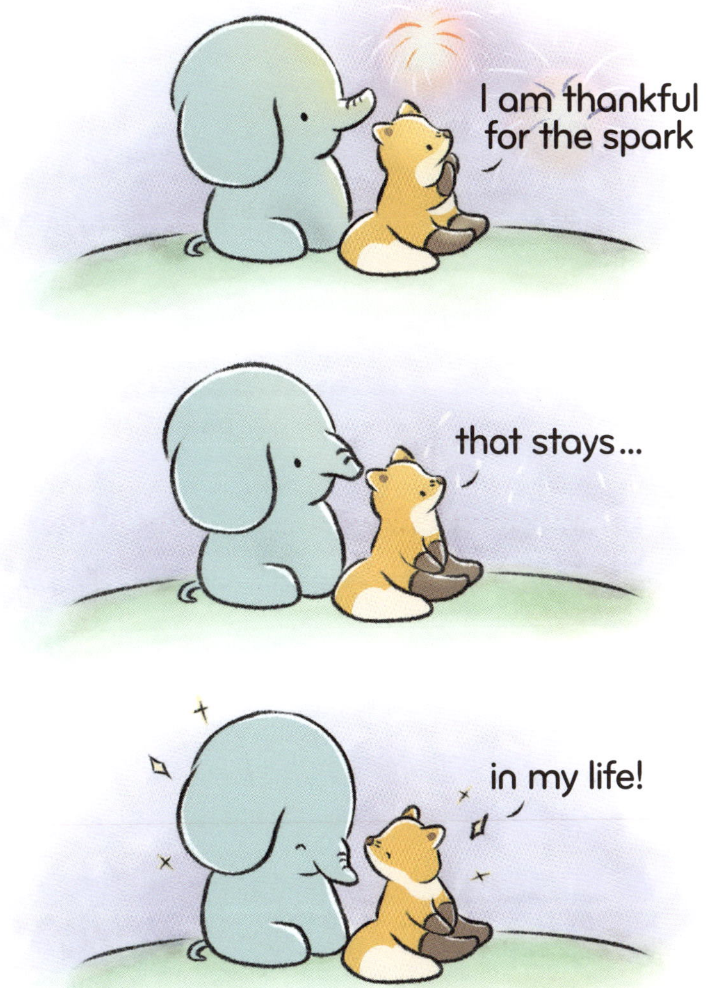
I am thankful
for the spark
that stays...
in my life!

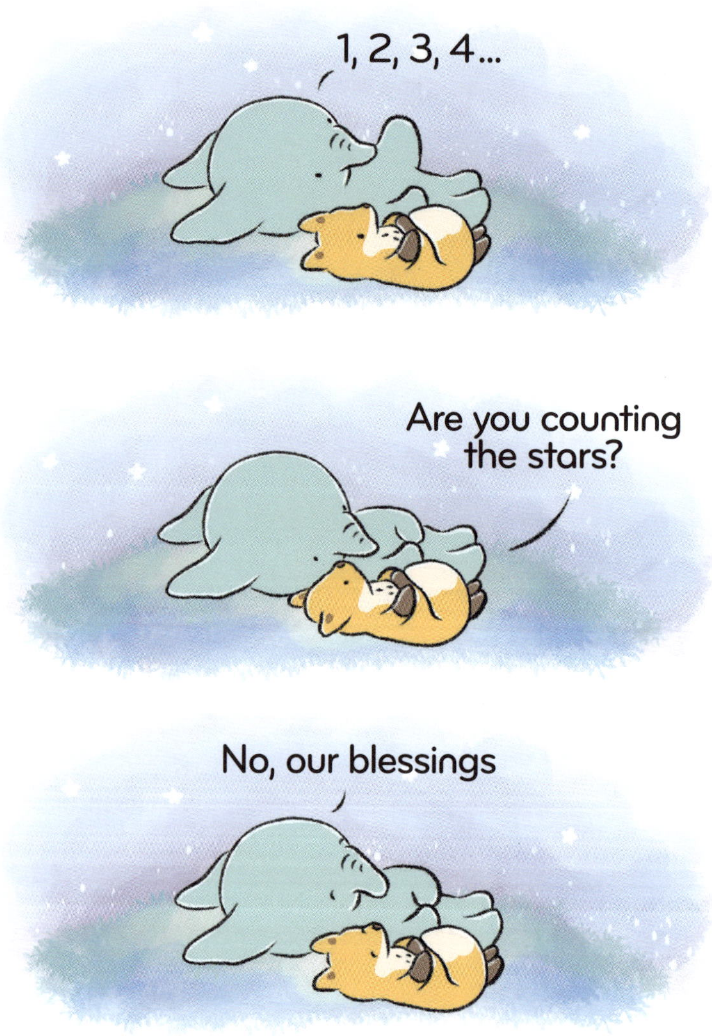
1, 2, 3, 4...
Are you counting the stars?
No, our blessings

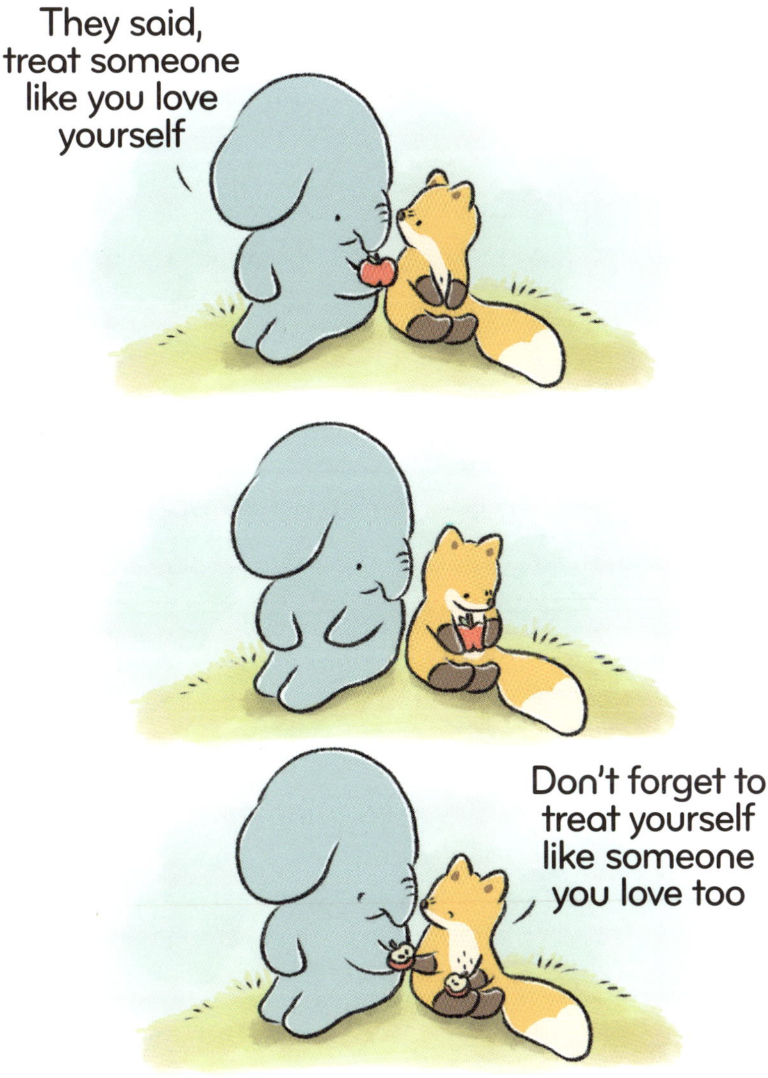
They said,
treat someone
like you love
yourself
Don't forget to
treat yourself
like someone
you love too

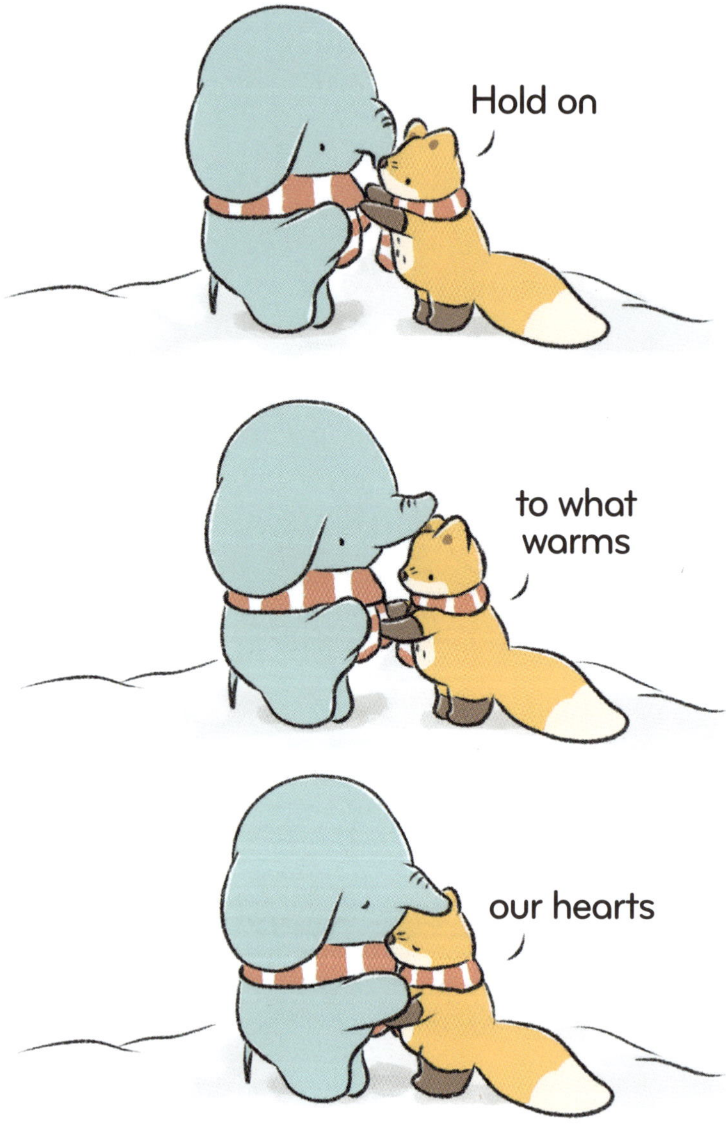
Hold on
to what
warms
our hearts

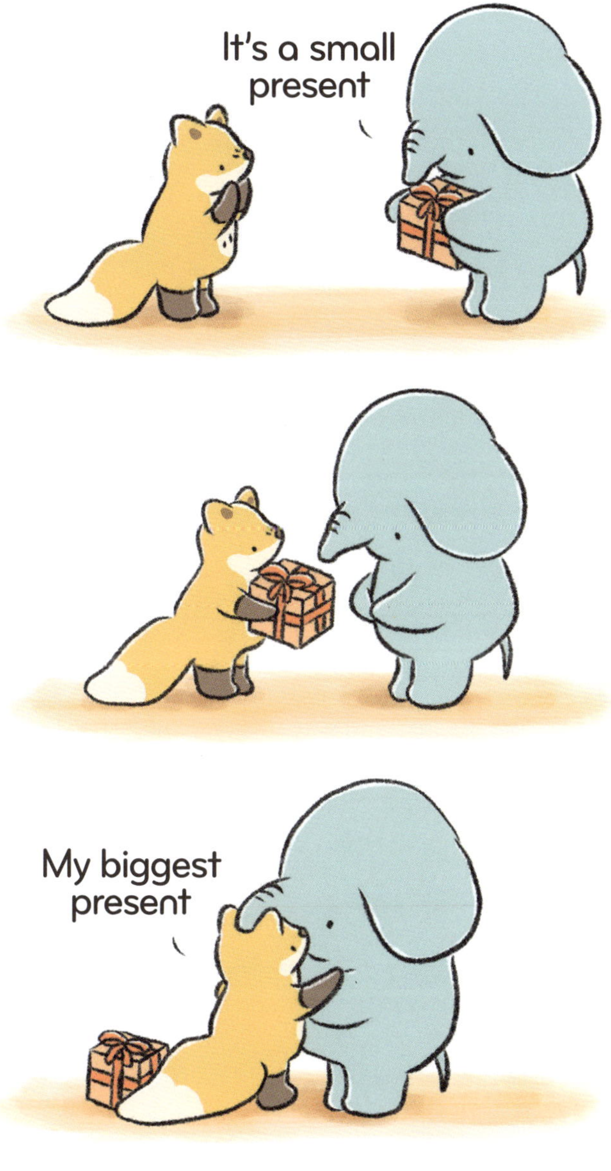
It's a small present
My biggest present

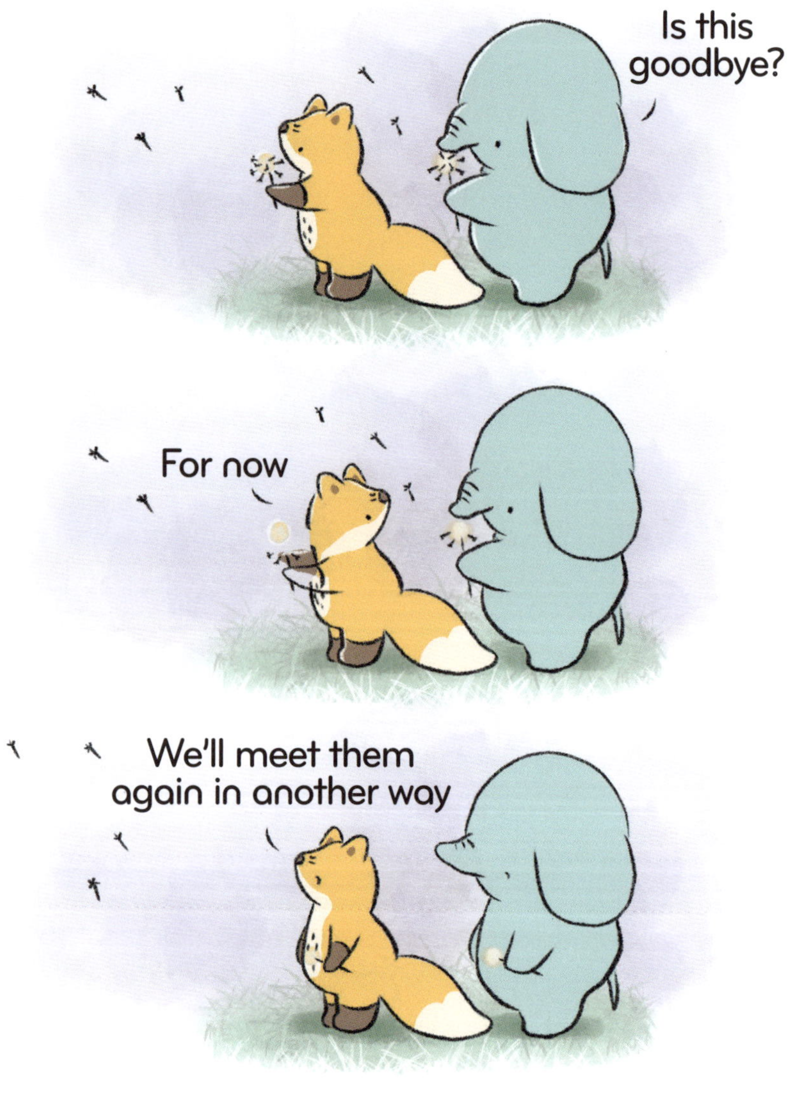
Is this goodbye?
For now
We'll meet them again in another way

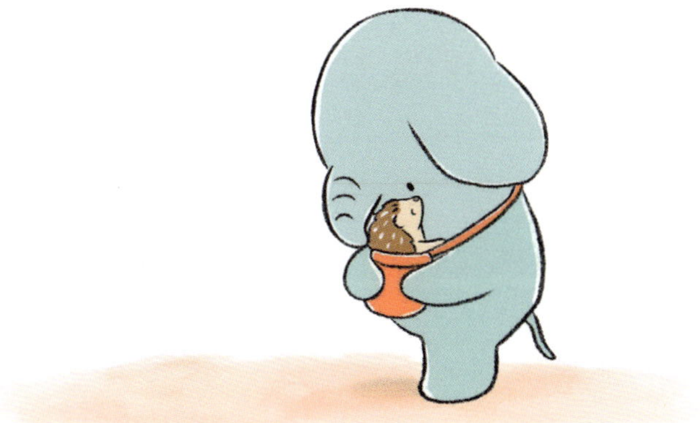

Hello there!

This is Fox

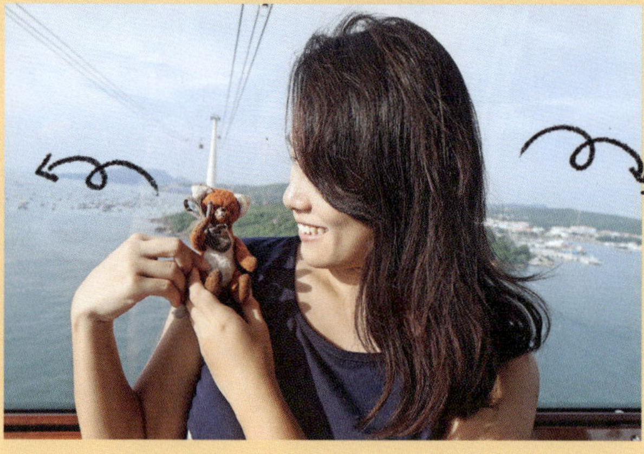

This is me

I'm Joanne Ang, or Jang, a self-taught children's book illustrator from Singapore and the creator of cosy webcomic JangandFox. Since 2018, I've been drawing cute animals to capture the simple, tender thoughts, inspirations and conversations around me.

During the COVID-19 pandemic, these comics were embraced by readers, psychologists and organisations to offer a reminder of human connection and mental health. At their heart, these childlike illustrations are small offerings of hope and companionship for anyone going through a tricky day!

My greatest teacher in empathy has been my mum, who has faced life's toughest challenges with grace and kindness. When I'm not illustrating, you'll likely find me spending quiet, unhurried moments with loved ones, painting, penning a letter, drafting song lyrics, or volunteering as a barber or a befriender.

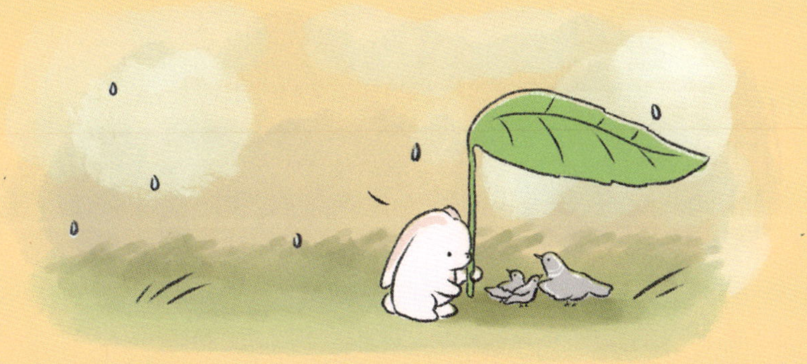

HarperCollins*Publishers*
1 London Bridge Street
London SE1 9GF

www.harpercollins.co.uk

HarperCollins*Publishers*
Macken House, 39/40 Mayor Street Upper
Dublin 1, D01 C9W8, Ireland

First published by HarperCollins*Publishers* 2025

10 9 8 7 6 5 4 3 2 1

A catalogue record of this book is available from the British Library

ISBN 978-0-00-872538-9

Printed and bound by GPS